The Critical Idiom

Founder Editor: JOHN D. JUMP (1969–1976)

21 Comedy

Comedy / *Moelwyn Merchant*

Methuen

LONDON and NEW YORK

First published 1972
by Methuen & Co. Ltd
11 New Fetter Lane, London EC4P 4EE
Reprinted twice
Reprinted 1980

Published in the USA by
Methuen & Co.
in association with Methuen, Inc.
733 Third Avenue, New York, NY 10017

© 1972 Moelwyn Merchant

Printed in Great Britain
by J. W. Arrowsmith Ltd, Bristol

ISBN 0 416 75050 8

Contents

General Editor's Preface

The volumes composing the Critical Idiom deal with a wide variety of key terms in our critical vocabulary. The purpose of the series differs from that served by the standard glossaries of literary terms. Many terms are adequately defined for the needs of students by the brief entries in these glossaries, and such terms do not call for attention in the present series. But there are other terms which cannot be made familiar by means of compact definitions. Students need to grow accustomed to them through simple and straightforward but reasonably full discussions. The main purpose of this series is to provide such discussions.

Many critics have borrowed methods and criteria from currently influential bodies of knowledge or belief that have developed without particular reference to literature. In our own century some of them have drawn on art-history, psychology, or sociology. Others, strong in a comprehensive faith, have looked at literature and literary criticism from a Marxist or a Christian or some other sharply defined point of view. The result has been the importation into literary criticism of terms from the vocabularies of these sciences and creeds. Discussions of such bodies of knowledge and belief in their bearing upon literature and literary criticism form a natural extension of the initial aim of the Critical Idiom.

Because of their diversity of subject-matter, the studies in the series vary considerably in structure. But all authors have tried to give as full illustrative quotation as possible, to make reference whenever appropriate to more than one literature, and to write in such a way as to guide readers towards the short bibliographies in which they have made suggestions for further reading.

University of Manchester   John D. Jump

Prefatory Note

There is scarcely need to apologize for omissions from a book of something over twenty-thousand words on a topic as teasing and as wide-ranging as *Comedy*. But some of the omissions should none the less be noted. Major writers of comedy – Terence and Plautus, most of the Elizabethans – are missing; Spanish, Russian and German comedy are rarely mentioned; drama is concentrated upon almost to the exclusion of the novel. I have chosen rather to analyse particular moments in the theatre as examples of a comic mode, allowing the critical analogies and parallels to be deduced by the reader. It would have been interesting to have explored the change in society and in sensibility that establishes the gulf between 'social comedy' in Congreve and Wycherley and in Goldsmith and Sheridan; to have explored the witty sickness of Wilde. Such a social anthropology, treated only in outline, would have demanded a book twice the length of any in this series; a similar volume would have been needed to place even the major critical theorists in relation to each other.

Little of this has been attempted; rather this essay tries to move towards a 'definition' of comedy by accumulating critical judgements. This may do something to avoid the dilemmas into which more general *a priori* theories of comedy have so regularly fallen.

My debts are numerous: to Eluned Brown of the University of Edinburgh for so much generously stimulating criticism; to Christopher Fry whose practice of tragedy and comedy lies behind much of this argument; to my son-in-law David Shaw of the Department of French in the University of Leeds and my son

Paul Merchant of the University of Tennessee, who both taught me to avoid certain traps and provided me with material and with translations from French and the Classics; and to my wife for so much assistance and for preparing the index. A particular debt is owed to Professor Robert W. Corrigan, whose valuable anthology, *Comedy: Meaning and Form,* stimulated much of my argument.

And above all to the Editor, John Jump, to whose kindly expertise patience has been added in such boundless measure.

My dedication expresses a debt which is long-standing and happy.

I

The Status of Comedy

> The most lamentable comedy and most
> cruel death of Pyramus and Thisby.

The 'mechanicals' in *A Midsummer Night's Dream* are no more
confused in their categories than most of the theorists and critics
who have concerned themselves with the nature of comedy; for
the conjunction of 'lamentable comedy' and 'cruel death' is a
permanently recurring affront to the purity of comedy and
tragedy as dramatic categories. The intrusion of laughter at the
moment of tragic revelation; the porter's boisterous perception
that, located in Macbeth's castle, he ministers at hell's gate; the
'tragic exit' of Shylock as prelude to radiance in Belmont; the
bawdy irony of Lear's fool; the absurd inarticulacy of a character in
Pinter or Beckett: all these deny the clarity with which the critical
intelligence from Aristotle onwards has tried to keep tragedy and
comedy in proper isolation, in appropriate antithesis. For the
assumed opposition of tragic and comic is no mere balance of
genres; writers both critical and creative in every age have set up
antitheses that assume more than a formal difference in literary
kinds between them. Byron describes a ritual and ceremonial
contrast as their fundamental distinction:

> All tragedies are finished by a death,
> All comedies are ended by a marriage,
>
> (*Don Juan*)

an entry into a profound area of human experience in which the
poet anticipates the 'ritualistic critics' of today. Horace Walpole

looks not to a ritual conclusion but to the level and quality of comprehension involved in comic and tragic experience:

> The world is a comedy to those that think, a tragedy to those that feel.

In the give and take of urbane conversation this convenient distinction may pass and – urbanely – we may refrain from pressing the emotional force of *Twelfth Night* or *Tartuffe*, the rational power of *Macbeth* or *Phèdre*; 'those that think' are manifestly capable of sensibility, 'those that feel' of powerful thought. But be that as it may, critics and belletristes have assumed that wit and sensibility, ratiocination and intuition, cool analysis and warm sympathy are among the contrasted means whereby the realms of comedy and tragedy are entered; and already we may suspect that they are being placed in an order of preference, a hierarchy of esteem.

Ben Jonson establishes a third category of difference when, in *Every Man in his Humour*, he distinguishes between the proper subject matter of comedy and tragedy:

> And persons, such as *Comœdie* would chuse,
> When she would shew an Image of the times,
> And sport with humane follies, not with crimes.
> Except, we make 'hem such by loving still
> Our popular errors, when we know th'are ill.
> I meane such errors, as you'll all confesse
> By laughing at them, they deserve no lesse:
> Which when you heartily doe, there's hope left, then,
> You, that have so grac'd monsters, may like men.
>
> *(Folio of 1616*

This is a plausible distinction, between 'follies' and 'crimes' though insistent doubts concerning Sir Epicure Mammon an Tribulation Wholesome question the moment at which a foible, 'humour' becomes something profounder and darker. Elsewhere in the critical prose of *Timber, or Discoveries*, Jonson anxiousl maintains the essential seriousness of *both* genres:

The parts of a Comedie are the same with a *Tragedie*, and the end is partly the same. For, they both delight, and teach: the *Comicks* are called διδάσχαλοι, of the *Greekes*; no lesse then the *Tragicks*.

Nor, is the moving of laughter alwaies the end of *Comedy*, that is rather a fowling for the peoples delight, or their fooling. For, as *Aristotle* saies rightly, the moving of laughter is a fault in Comedie, a kind of turpitude, that depraves some parts of a mans nature without a disease.

Yet this stressing of the didactic quality in both comedy and tragedy fails to mask the distinction which Jonson himself notes in his creative intention: that comedy is concerned with the foolish, with social aberrations, while tragedy handles 'crime', a rebellion against a profounder ethic. Here we appear to have set up a qualitative distinction and are invited to admit that the gravity of comedy, even when it refrains from ticklish laughter, is, in its ultimate moral concern, in some sort less than that of tragedy. Jonson seems to be starting a line of critical vocabulary in which the metaphors carry judgements of value; tragedy is regularly associated with 'profundity', 'gravity', 'density of involvement', 'earnestness'; comedy with 'mirth', 'levity', 'wit', 'the sunny malice of a faun' – the contrasts are sufficiently revealing, even if their implications are not often explored. Nor do Jonson's successors who seek to redress the critical balance, emphasizing the salutary social function of comedy, always arouse full confidence: Meredith's 'thoughtful laughter' is as disconcerting as Hazlitt's contrary tone in his distinction between Shakespearian comedy and tragedy:

He was greatest in what was greatest [tragedy]; and his *forte* was not trifling.

This juxtaposition of 'greatest' and 'trifling' is a forthright declaration that the status of tragedy is in itself higher than comedy; and indeed an audience may well feel that it is about a graver business when it assists at a tragic performance than when it 'relaxes' in the presence of comedy. An analogous assumption may be heard obliquely in the tone of a puritan in 1600 as he characterizes 'romish' liturgical practices:

> Their comedicall dancing masses, skipping and hopping about the altar like apes,

while even in his sober assessment of comedy in the *Apology*, Sidney makes no more powerful a claim than that it is 'an imitation of the common errors of our life', those follies which in Jonsonian terms are so much less reprehensible than crimes.

Yet it will be the argument of this essay that there are critical standpoints from which it would seem that comedy has a nobler metaphysical quality than these traditional tones and phrases would imply; that particular comedies in our Western literatures have attitudes which go beyond this mildly therapeutic role, the mere chastisement of folly; that Aristophanes, Shakespeare, Molière or Brecht provide us with teasing problems of evaluation if we attempt to confine their comedy simply to social correction.

But we must begin our exploration of the genre with dictionary definition, if this 'Critical Idiom' is to be pursued into the proper sphere of practical criticism. Even here we are not on completely unambiguous ground, for the *O.E.D.* derives the noun from *comædia*, in turn from the Greek Κωμῶδια 'either of Κῶμος, a revel, merrymaking, or of its probable source Κώμη, village ἀοιδός, singer, minstrel ... The Κωμωζός was thus originally either "the bard of the revels" or "the village bard"' – a not insignificant distinction in itself. This ambiguity in the very derivation of the word is continued in the *O.E.D.* citations of early use in illustration of its question-begging definition: 'A stage play of a light and amusing character with a happy conclusion to the plot' the *Chronicle of Troy* (1430) has in fact a subtler definition than this in denying its uniformly 'light and amusing character':

A comedy hath in his gynnynge, [beginning]
A pryme face, a maner complaynguage,
And afterward endeth in gladnesse,

while Chaucer, in *Troylus and Criseyde*, half a century earlier, marks the conclusion of his work:

Go, litel bok, go, litel myne tragedye,
Ther God thi makere yet, er that he dye,
So sende myght to maken som comedye!

Shakespeare – or at least his first editors in the *Folio* of 1623 – was in the same ambivalence of mind over this 'sour comedy', this 'tragical history' or 'comical satire' of Troilus and Cressida's love. The significance, however, of the passage from Chaucer in our present exploration is the interesting order and relationship, that with God's help he will be sent 'myght to maken som comedye'. It would be hazardous and unbalanced to press the argument too far but it is certainly a modest and justifiable conclusion that the progress from tragedy to comedy (from *Troylus* to the *Canterbury Tales*?) was for Chaucer in no sense an anticlimax, a movement from a serious game to mere literary trifling. To return for a moment to the dictionary definition: the first sub-definition reads, 'a mediaeval narrative poem with an agreeable ending cf. Dante'. It is certainly no over-statement to regard the cosmic sequence from Inferno to Paradiso by way of Purgatorio as a progress towards 'an agreeable ending'; Dante's poetic achievement of the beatific vision, after the 'secular' powers of Vergil had taken him to the limit of insight granted to human reason, gives the most substantial ground for the subsequent nature of comedy, an intellectual and spiritual standpoint which gives the literary form its claim to insights as grave and weighty as those of tragedy.

These considerations seem largely to have turned on the question of status – the relative esteem in which tragedy and comedy are held. For, apart from particular plays – which rates the highest, the author of *The Frogs* or of *Lear*, of *Volpone* or *Phèdre*, of *Twelfth Night* or *Brand*? – there appears to be the begged question, that it is nobler to be a tragedian than a comedian, that to be tragic is to participate in sublimity, to be comic is to have affinity with the pitiable. These questions, whether posed or begged, have overtones, intellectual and emotional, which imply the teasing doubt whether the apparently simple question, 'what is comedy?' is in fact a question of critical theory, of psychology, of sociology or of metaphysics. We shall not escape, in following our inquiry from involvement in all these abstractions – though from some of them we shall seek a hurried disengagement.

2

Psychological Theories of Comedy

The sources of comedy – and sometimes simply of 'the comic' – have been sought in psychological states, in myth and ritual and in 'sociological' accounts which deem comic literature valuable because in some way therapeutic. It would probably be most useful to begin the search for origins where in fact dictionary definition began: with the beginnings of classical comedy and with Satyr plays; but it has been so fashionable during the past fifty years to begin with the psychological basis of comedy – to cite Sigmund Freud on laughter and Henri Bergson on 'le monde renversé' – that it seems as well to clear this obstacle before pursuing a more profitable course.

We may none the less begin with a proper warning. L. C. Knights in his 'Notes on Comedy' (*The Importance of Scrutiny*, London, 1964) fastens on the central fallacy of the psychological exploration of a literary mode, its commitment to abstraction and generalization as opposed to the proper business of criticism, the delicate pursuit of particulars. 'Once an invariable connection between comedy and laughter is assumed we are not likely to make any observation that will be useful as criticism. We have only to find the formula that will explain laughter, and we know the 'secret' of Jonson and Rabelais, Chaucer and Fielding, Jane Austen and Joyce ... None of [the solutions to the problem of laughter] will help us to become better because more responsive readers of Molière' (p. 227). Yet in every symposium on Comedy the search persists for such a formula and some of the conclusions must be examined, if only to recognize them as critical dead-ends.

We may begin with some oblique psychology, fresh, valuable

and unprofessional. Mack Sennett (and who had more right to pronounce a grave dictum?) declared as a working principle: 'The joke of life is the fall of dignity.' By an apposite incongruity we find Sennett and one of our most distinguished theologians, Niebuhr, exploring adjacent mental territory (Niebuhr cited in Martin Gardner's introduction to *The Annotated Alice*, Harmondsworth, 1965, p. 15):

> Laughter, declared Reinhold Niebuhr in one of his finest sermons, is a kind of no man's land between faith and despair. We preserve our sanity by laughing at life's surface absurdities, but the laughter turns to bitterness and derision is directed towards the deeper irrationalities of evil and death. 'That is why,' he concludes, 'there is laughter in the vestibule of the temple, the echo of laughter in the temple itself, but only faith and prayer, and no laughter, in the holy of holies.'

'The fall of dignity', 'life's surface absurdities', 'the deeper irrationalities of evil and death' – these are the facts, of ascending intensity, in face of which a great comic genius and an influential theologian see comedy as effective – or, in the final analysis, impotent – in preserving our sanity. Sennett, Chaplin, Harold Lloyd, the Marx Brothers, the classical figures of the silent film and the early days of 'talkies', applied the therapy of laughter to certain absurdities and irrationalities; it now remains to question whether psychological categories can profitably extend the relations of laughter and comedy in the borderland between faith and despair, between absurdity and evil, in which the theologian and the literary critic both move of necessity.

It is customary to begin an examination of the relation between laughter and comedy with Freud, whose *Jokes and their Relation to the Unconscious* is its classical statement. Eric Bentley (in *The Life of the Drama*, London, 1965) summarizes the central significance of Freud's analysis of laughter:

> Gilbert Murray has spoken of the 'close similarity between Aristotle and Freud', and actually Freud carried the idea of Catharsis further

than any Aristotelian commentator had ever dreamt of. In the eighteen-nineties the new therapy escaped being named cathartic instead of psycho-analytic only by a hair's breadth. For Freud, jokes are fundamentally cathartic: a release, not a stimulant.

(p. 237)

Bentley, however, recognizes that this is the simple beginning of Freudian theory on laughter and that further distinctions which have relation to comedy and farce in the theatre are relevant:

> Freud distinguishes two kinds of jokes, one which is innocent and harmless, and one which has a purpose, a tendency, an end in view. He distinguishes in turn two kinds of purpose: to destroy and to expose – to smash and to strip. Destructive jokes fall under such headings as sarcasm, scandal, and satire, denuding jokes under such headings as obscenity, bawdry, ribaldry.

(p. 245)

These distinctions are of course no more than logically valid; as soon as they are transferred to the business of criticizing a particular play, they become blurred. Bentley shrewdly remarks that even as distinctions they are surprising; 'the only startling thing about this classification is that it places obscenity side by side with satire'. But when it comes to actualities of the stage, 'there is destructive force also in the joke that exposes'. Indeed one might say that if it is appropriate to use the term 'joke' in this context, the exposure of Malvolio is a joke that potentially destroys; the exposure of Shylock to the full process of justice overturns his world; in either event we are forced beyond the boundaries where the comic is coterminous with the jocular.

Freud himself has given some attention to the theatrically comic effect of incongruity, particularly the disparity between effort and result:

> A person appears comic to us if, in comparison with ourselves, he makes too great an expenditure on his bodily functions and too little

on his mental ones; and it cannot be denied that in both these cases our laughter expresses a pleasurable sense of this superiority which we feel in relation to him.

(*Jokes and their Relation to the Unconscious*, 1960, James Strachey, p. 195)

Hence our laughter at the antics of a clown, which seem to us 'extravagant and inexpedient'. But once more we are faced with the inadequacy of a psychological theory when it is transferred to the realm of art and its criticism. There is 'extravagance' in Malvolio's thirst for social advancement, in Shylock's determination to be avenged on Antonio; there are elements of the comic-grotesque in their self-revelation and there is a mode of comedy in our wry recognition of their absurdity when we observe Malvolio cross-gartered in the service of his love or Shylock stropping his knife while the trial proceeds. But there is an overspill, a pressure here which makes 'extravagant and inexpedient' a wholly inadequate phrase to account for our complex reactions – and it would be an insensitive observer who found the sentences 'I'll be revenged on the whole pack of you' and 'give me leave to go from hence; I am not well' mere extensions of the sardonic humour with which Malvolio and Shylock are for the most part observed.

With Henri Bergson the psychology of the comic becomes the basis for examining the comic theatre; in *Laughter. An Essay on the Meaning of the Comic* (trs. 1911, Brereton and Rothwell) he explores the nature of the comic situation as it becomes the subject matter of drama:

Picture to yourselves certain characters in a certain situation; if you reverse the situation and invert the roles, you obtain a comic scene . . The plot of the villain who is the victim of his own villainy, or the cheat cheated, forms the stock-in-trade of a good many plays . . . in every case the root idea involves an inversion of roles, and a situation which recoils on the head of the author.

At the level of farce this is clearly valid and it may result in subtl social comment; Laurel and Hardy and the Marx Brothers wholly mastered this form of comedy. But once more we have to estimate the particular validity of a general psychological theory: *The Merchant of Venice* is brought to the brink of tragic insight precisely by this 'reversal of roles' in the fourth act; furthermore, Bergson's definition is adequately applied to *peripeteia*, the source of most tragic denouement. One part of our mind may stand back in wry comment on the irony of fate which produces such reversal as to lead to complete catastrophe – but the ironic smile is at some distance removed from the laughter of comedy. Do we even smile at the tragic ironies of Oedipus?

Finally there is the more fruitful and suggestive area of psychological argument concerning dramatic modes which relates comedy (and tragedy) to those areas of the unconscious where archetypal images preside. Martin Grotjahn (in *Beyond Laughter*, New York, 1957) has expressed very adequately certain fundamental situations of this kind as they emerge to consciousness in comedy:

> When Freud discovered the unconscious during his great creative period, he found also in the Oedipus situation the genuine meaning of all great human tragedy: the infatuation with the mother, the taboo of incest, the rebellion of the son against the tyrannical father, the guilt and punishment by castration for the crime in thought or action, conscious or unconscious.
>
> (p. 258)

Allowing for the exaggeration in the phrase 'all great human tragedy', we may accept the truth in that stereotype. Grotjahn goes on to explore the reverse situation:

> The psychodynamics of the comedy can be understood as a kind of reversed Oedipus situation in which the son does not rebel against the father but the son's typical attitudes of childhood longing are projected upon the father. The son plays the role of the victorious father with sexual freedom and achievement, while the father is cast in the role of the frustrated onlooker. The reversed Oedipus situation

is repeated in every man's life when the younger generation grows up and slowly infiltrates and replaces the older generation in work and in life. The clown is the comic figure representing the impotent and ridiculed father.

(p. 259)

As a pattern this is interesting and suggestive but Grotjahn concludes with an extension of the clown's role by which he makes his most valuable critical point:

[The clown] also represents the sadness of things and finally comes to stand for death in the person of the tragic, truly great clown. This is the point when tragedy and comedy finally meet and symbolize human life.

It is remarkable how this study returns again and again to the inevitable intersection of comedy and tragedy. Indeed, when the psychologists have had their proper say, it is left to the literary critic, working delicately within the particular text, to show this intermixture of comedy and tragedy at its most searing. G. Wilson Knight, in a brilliant chapter, 'King Lear and the Comedy of the Grotesque' in *The Wheel of Fire*, thus locates this meeting-point

This particular region of the terrible bordering on the fantastic and absurd is exactly the playground of madness . . . The gouging out of Gloucester's eyes is a thing unnecessary, crude, disgusting: it is meant to be. It helps to provide an accompanying exaggeration of one element – that of cruelty – in the horror that makes Lear's madness And not only horror: there is even again something satanically comic bedded deep in it. The sight of physical torment, to the uneducated brings laughter. Shakespeare's England delighted in watching both physical torment and the comic ravings of actual lunacy. The dance of madmen in Webster's *Duchess of Malfi* is of the same ghoulish humour as Regan's plucking Gloucester by the beard: the groundling will laugh at both.

(pp. 168–9)

3
The Classical World

It might be supposed that the classical origins of comedy, both in the plays of the Greeks and in their admirably logical and categorized literary-critical theories, would provide us with philosophic notions which would separate more precisely the mode of comedy from that of tragedy. We should still of course, however clear the categories, be faced with those high moments of which Wilson Knight wrote in the last quotation, where the two worlds modify each other, and we should still be faced with the dilemma of the writer himself, of which Christopher Fry has said:

> When I set about writing a comedy the idea presents itself first of all as tragedy. The characters press on to the theme with all their divisions and perplexities heavy about them . . . If the characters were not qualified for tragedy there would be no comedy, and to some extent I have to cross the one before I can light on the other.

This is a practical affirmation, the experience of the writer concerned with the actualities of drama and not with the abstract distinctions of genre: out of the experience comes a further affirmation, metaphysical in its import:

> Somehow the characters have to unmortify themselves: to affirm life and assimilate death and persevere in joy . . . The *Book of Job* is the great reservoir of comedy: 'But there is a spirit in man . . . the blessing of him that was ready to perish came upon me; and I caused the widow's heart to sing for joy.'

If Fry sees *Job* as 'a reservoir of comedy' while Wilson Knight finds 'something satanically comic bedded deep' in the tragedy of *Lear*, we may well have to look to profounder levels than usual in order to evaluate these moments when tragedy and comedy meet. Greek drama hints at some of those levels.

The Greek theatre is usually perfectly happy to mix tragedy with comedy and with deliberate, contrived and subtle effects. As we should expect, Euripides among the major dramatists is the boldest in counter-posing the two modes and his *Alcestis* is among the most complex examples in its range. But Euripides was not in this respect a revolutionary and we shall find mature examples of the relation of comedy and tragedy in both Aeschylus and Sophocles. Indeed it is probably just to say that we shall penetrate most deeply into the genre of comedy by first exploring its creative relationship with tragedy in the Greek theatre and exploring its analogies in the Shakespearian.

It is convenient to analyse these intrusions into tragedy by way of three comic modes, those of farce, of dramatic humour and of satire. Like all critical distinctions, these are rarely in practice wholly separable and they frequently merge; farce is rarely without ironic satire, when associated with the heightened tension of tragedy; humour (especially in the form of 'comic relief') never without its overtones of critical irony.

Farce is normally the preserve of the fourth play in a tetralogy, the satyr-play (a convenient and available example is the *Cyclops*) where it is of major feature in the final cathartic process extending through the four plays. But it is by no means absent from the preceding tragedies themselves (and we shall find later that Marlowe in *The Jew of Malta* is heir to this classical tradition: the play is called a tragedy on its title-page but its dominant mode is a sardonic farce rising to savage intensity). One of the best examples of the intrusion of farcical comedy into a tragic situation is found in the *Helen* of Euripides and it has the added interest of being the subject of a parody by Aristophanes within a very few years (*Helen* was produced in 412 B.C., the *Thermophoriazusae* of Aristophanes in 411 or 410). The intensity of mood in the *Helen* may best be assessed by contrast with a characteristic scene from a satyr-play, the *Cyclops* of Euripides. In most of the satyr-plays the comedy, as befits a concluding farce, is more of situation than of verbal brilliance but there is a characteristic, crude verbalizing which takes the place of wit, without ever rising to the rich in-consequentiality and absurdity (to say nothing of the sheer verbal ingenuity) of Aristophanes.

Lines 669–75 of *Cyclops* focus this farcical word-play. Poly-phemus, blinded by Odysseus calling himself Nobody is ques-tioned by a chorus of satyrs:

> *Chorus* What are you shouting about, Cyclops? *Cyclops* I'm dead.
> *Chorus* You mean deadly. *Cyclops* Dead to the world.
> *Chorus* Dead drunk and you fell in the fire.
> *Cyclops* I was battered by Nobody. *Chorus* Then nobody touched you.
> *Cyclops* Nobody blinded me. *Chorus* Then you can see
> *Cyclops* If you were in my place – *Chorus* What? Blinded by nobody?
> *Cyclops* Don't fool me; where's Nobody? *Chorus* Nowhere, Cyclops.

The rhythmic drive of this passage can be seen even in translation: played merely farcically the passage could have a cheap flatness, but the verbal wit associated with the cruel calamity of blinding makes farce here to a higher power. We are inevitably led to a comparison with the tragic farce of Lear's mad wit as he comments to Gloucester on his blindness:

> I remember thine eyes well enough; dost thou squiny at me? No, do thy worst, blind Cupid, I'll not love ... No eyes in your head, nor no money in your purse? Your eyes are in a heavy case, your purse in a light, yet you see how this world goes.

> (IV. vi.)

It is a far cry from *Cyclops* to *King Lear* but the farcical-flyting mode applied to the cruel suffering of blindness brings the satyr-comedy into close association with mature tragedy.

The non-verbal aspects of farce can be illustrated in a brief scene from *Helen*. Here we find the cumulative effect of incongruity piled on incongruity, characteristic of farce. Menelaus arrives in Egypt after the Trojan war, bringing with him Helen – but her image or phantasm only, over which ironically the war had been fought; for the real Helen had been throughout the struggle in the keeping of Proteus, king of Egypt. Leaving his spirit-Helen in a sea-cave, Menelaus comes inland and there finds the real Helen. Euripides treats us to what can only be called a burlesque of the recognition-scenes that are normally such a fine feature of Greek drama; in this scene he clearly relishes the opportunities for humour in Menelaus's bewilderment and adds to the comedy by the visual device of bringing Menelaus on to the stage in a tattered, sea-weedy costume. The farce leads to inarticulate comedy:

Menelaus I find you incredibly like Helen, lady.
Helen And you like Menelaus. I don't know what to say.

There is little need to comment on the backward-reflecting irony, on the whole tragic comedy of the Trojan war fought over a phantasm, as this farcical encounter adds a coda to the years of suffering. Within two years of the play's performance on the tragic stage Aristophanes included a version of this scene in his *Thermophoriazusae*, borrowing many of Euripides's lines verbatim, some indication of the complexity of contemporary audience reaction to the original tragedy.

With the second mode of the classical theatre's association of comedy with tragedy, we have been made very familiar by its Shakespearian use. The interpolation of comic scenes immediately before or after moments of extreme tragic tension has been described, with unconscious critical irony, as 'comic relief': the countryman with the asps, as Cleopatra prepares for death, Macbeth's porter, 'devil-portering' at the very gates of hell, the 'antic disposition' of Hamlet after the murder of Polonius. It is

fact an occasion both for the physical release of tension in laughter
– the startled gasp as the knocking thunders on the gate of Dunsinane – and a counter-heightening of tragic tension, in preparation
for the next turn of the screw. There are important examples in
the Greek theatre. Early in Sophocles's *Antigone* the tragic dilemma
of the play is established, that two moralities are in conflict: the
'piety' of Antigone with the necessity of burying her brother, and
the positive edict of Creon that he be left unburied. The entry of
Antigone is prepared by the comedy of the sentry:

> *Sentry* Your Majesty, there is no such thing as a certainty; you lay
> your bet, and when you turn round, you've lost it. I went away
> from here just now swearing I wouldn't come back for another dose
> of your royal temper, but here I am – still, there's nothing I like
> better than a surprise winner, that's what I say; so, oath or no oath,
> I'm back. I've got the girl. She did it; we caught her burying him.
> There was no dicing for this job; I had the luck to catch her, and so
> I've brought her along. I'll leave her to you now, sir; you can get
> the facts from her. I'm glad to see the end of the whole business. I
> can't say I enjoyed it.
> *Creon* Do you realise who this is? Where did you find her?
> *Sentry* I've told you already, she was burying him.

This is by no means a scene of 'comic relief'. The vulgarity of the
sentry's tone is given consistency and a 'comic' propriety by the
skill with which Antigone's tragic act of duty is reduced to gam-
bling terms: 'a certainty', 'your bet', 'a surprise winner', 'no dicing'.
The tragedy is devalued to the point of the sentry's brooding
words, 'the end of the whole business'. This tone is picked up
ironically by Creon: 'Do you realise who this is?'; for the identity
of Antigone marks the beginning not the end of the tragic affair.

The technique of this passage from Sophocles should be contrasted with another comic interlude in the *Bacchae* of Euripides.
At lines 912–76 Dionysus dresses Pentheus as a woman so that he
can spy on the Bacchic rituals of the Theban maenads. The scene

is clearly written with great care and attention to detail (there appear to be even occasional instances of rhyme, extremely rare in Greek drama) and, as in *Antigone*, the moment of comedy precedes a moment of great tragic tension. Here the burlesque is the immediate prologue to the description of the ritual murder of Pentheus. The humour of the full scene is on more than one level; visually it borders on farce as Pentheus is dressed as a woman for the exploit of spying; it suggests sexual motivation with its ribald associations as Pentheus eagerly anticipates his observation of the maenad rituals; and finally there is pure irony (at lines 961–2 when, having fully assumed the *female* disguise, Pentheus boasts:

> Lead me straight through the land of Thebes;
> I'm the only one of them *man* enough for this:

Most essentially Greek of all these comic modes is the third, dramatic irony properly so-called, as opposed to its incidental intrusion, as in the last example from the *Bacchae*. There is a fine moment in Aeschylus's *Agamemnon* (at lines 606–10) in which Clytemnestra makes a bid for the support of the Chorus before the arrival of Agamemnon:

Clytemnestra Let him come and find his wife at home,
  Faithful as always, his house-dog
  True to him, a terror to his enemies,
  With nothing changed,
  No contract broken in all that time.

The irony here is not only in its manifest falsehood (clear to the audience but not to the Chorus) but also in the 'watch-dog' metaphor, contrasting with the moving description of Odysseus' dog Argus (in *Odyssey* 17), dying of joy at seeing his master's return. Even more to the point, it also echoes the words of Agamemnon himself when describing his murder to Odysseus in the Underworld (in *Odyssey* 11); here the word used strikingly to describe Clytemnestra is 'bitch'; Aeschylus is here, in 'house dog [bitch]', evoking an ironic response of some subtlety. The reflective laughter of the audience at Clytemnestra's transparent duplicity with the Chorus depends on a highly sophisticated literary tradition and a cultivated theatre public.

It is Sophocles, however, who made dramatic irony peculiarly his own, and nowhere more than in *Oedipus Tyrannus*. At lines 264–8 we find it at its fullest and with its greatest 'comic' potentiality:

> *Creon* So I shall fight for him – just as I would
> For my own father – yes, at any cost
> I will find and take the murderer
> Of Laius, son of Labdacus son of Polydorus
> Son of Cadmus son of Agenor.

The embarrassment felt by the audience at hearing a man pronounce a curse of such formality against himself, and involving the supreme irony of 'just as I would/for my own father' teeters on the very edge of laughter, just as Richard's interruption of Margaret's curse in *Richard the Third* is exactly the stuff of which comedy of a bizarre kind is made. The situation in *Oedipus Tyrannus* involves a by no means unrelieved tragic posture; indeed, like all the other examples taken here from the Greek theatre, the tragic fact is intensified by the unambiguous recognition of comic potentiality at its core. Equally the grotesque comedy of *Richard the Third* has a degree of the terrible precisely to the extent that it recognizes the tragic impulse derived from the person of Richard and his equivocal circumstances.

4
'Comic Relief'

We are now in a position to explore more fully the implications of the constantly recurring phrase 'comic relief'. We have already seen in Greek theatre the very various degrees of intensity experienced in tragic drama by the impinging of diverse aspects of the comic temper. It would be interesting to speculate, if we admit any critical validity to the term 'comic relief' (however delicately the word 'relief' be interpreted), whether a similar value could be attached by analogy to the term 'tragic relief'. (I have never seen it used; why not?) It would seem that momentary deflection of the tragic temper by comedy prepares for a further access of tragedy; does a tragic deflection of comedy attain the same result? A further examination of *The Merchant of Venice* is helpful here.

The matter of this comedy may be stated lightly and conventionally enough; a young man borrows a huge sum of money of a friend in order to woo a young woman who is rich, fair and virtuous (his own stated order); his friend in turn borrows it of a money-lender who imposes a ridiculous and apparently unenforceable bond of a pound of flesh. When an attempt is made to enforce the security, the machinations of the usurer are defeated and, in a lyrical fifth act, all lovers are united in happiness. This statement of the dramatic outline is just enough and 'places' the plot in the realm of simple romance. But Shakespeare's play is very recalcitrant to this reduction to a fairy-tale mode. In the first place the money-lender is a conscientious and (if his profile and accurate citations of scripture are an appropriate indication) a both learned and pious Jew. The clash with Antonio is a sincere clash of rac and creed. Further, Portia, the lady sought with such trouble and expense of fortune, is of far greater stature than would befit mere romantic comedy; her court-room clash with Shylock is conducted with high subtlety and a final appeal ('the quality of mercy') to the highest reaches of equity in human and divine law. Finally the defeat of Shylock is reached with an emotional intensity very rare in the early comedies:

> *Portia* Art thou contented, Jew? What dost thou say?
> *Shylock* I am content.
> *Portia*   Clerk, draw a deed of gift.
> *Shylock* I pray you give me leave to go from hence,
>   I am not well; send the deed after me
>   And I will sign it.
>
>   (IV. i.)

The audience is here aware that more tragic intensity has been simply condensed in these words than can properly be given full dramatic scope and development without shattering the bounds of comedy. Indeed it was sometimes felt in the nineteenth century that this was the proper end of the play and that to pass to the fifth act would be to trivialize the theme. But even to raise Shylock to a quasi-tragic power and to leave the issue there is to over-simplify. We might suppose that the brooding weight and gravity of the fourth act, the physical danger to Antonio, the witty skill of Portia and the final calamity of Shylock add edge to the happiness and resolution of the fifth act (a validation of my suggestion of 'tragic relief'); but the dramatist does not enter the world of radiance directly from the darkness of Shylock's exit, as he does not enter the world of tragic darkness from the 'comedy' of the porter of *Macbeth* or the countryman and his asps in *Antony and Cleopatra*. The world of romantic radiance is very real: there is music (and a metaphysic of music comprehensive enough to enlarge its sphere to embrace the young-eyed cherubims'); there is light shining like good deeds 'in a naughty world' and above all there is the joy of wit, laughter and the union of lovers. But the transition from the courtroom to this world of reconciliation is slow and ambiguous. There is first the laying of the final complication of the rings, a witty 'comedy of situation'; but far more important is the tone of the opening exchange in the fifth act between Lorenzo and Jessica:

> In such a night as this . . . Troilus . . . Cressid . . . Thisbe . . . Dido . . .
> Medea.

These are ill-starred examplars for lovers on a moonlit night! But the exchange goes further than this classical list:

> *Lorenzo*   In such a night
> Did Jessica *steal* from the wealthy Jew,
> And with an *unthrift* love did run from Venice
> As far as Belmont.
> *Jessica*   In such a night
> Did young Lorenzo swear he loved her well,
> *Stealing* her soul with many vows of faith
> And *ne'er a true one*.
>
>   (V. i.

This is of course the secure badinage of assured love; insecure love would not risk the wounds latent in the language. None the less this is not yet radiance; there is the strong reminder that Troilus, Cressida, Thisbe, Dido and Medea were also lovers and that with perfidy, tragic ill-fortune, treacherous forsaking, and witchcraft these lovers severally frustrated their love or were denied its joy. This dark tone, with some of its vocabulary – 'steal' and 'unthrift' – borrowed from the main plot which bordered so nearly on tragedy, reinforces the idiom of Shylock's exit and extends it in time, to add greater force to the final serenity of the play.

This is to say no more than that the dramatist – and the play-goer – is capable of contemplating, without feeling the desire to reconcile, two contrasting moods at the same time. It is of course possible that the author or audience finds a means of reconciling

the two modes of being; Christopher Fry indicates the possibility
in the essay already cited:

> There an angle of experience where the dark is distilled into light;
> either here or hereafter, in or out of time: where our tragic fate finds
> itself with perfect pitch, and goes straight to the key in which creation
> was composed. And comedy senses and reaches out to this experience.

This is the union of comic with tragic, of which certain moments
in medieval drama are the clearest examples. At their highest these
plays are neither naïve nor clumsy; indeed their ability to move
through very different areas of sensibility without doing violence
to their own unity is one of their most notable characteristics. In
the 'Towneley Cycle' two of the plays, by the 'Wakefield Master',
those concerned with the vision of the Shepherds and their visit to
the Manger of the Nativity carry the sophisticated union of
comedy and gravity to its furthest point. *Prima Pastorum* opens
with a plaint for poverty, a tragic and at the same time ruefully
comic account of the plight of the poor:

> All my shepe ar gone,
> I am not left oone,
> The rot has theym slane [slain],
>   Now beg I and borrow ...
> Withe purs penneles
> That makes this hevynes!
> Wo is me this distres
>   And has no helpyng.
>
> (ll. 24–7, 33–6)

their woes are momentarily alleviated by a great feast which, in
form and words, recalls the miraculous feeding of the thousands
Christ (for, among other hints, the shepherds gather the
remains into 'panyers' to give to poor men) and immediately after
this prelude of bounty, the nativity is announced by an angel, with
the command to go to Bethlehem. As they observe the star they

recall prophecies of the birth and the third shepherd recalls and
quotes (if haltingly as is proper) the fourth pastoral poem of Vergil
(which has traditionally been called 'The Messianic Eclogue'):

> Virgille in his poetre sayde in his verse
> Even thus by gramare as I shall reherse,
> Jam nova progenies coelo demittitur alto,
> Jam rediet virgo, redeunt Saturnia regna.
> (Now a young child descends from the lofty sky,
> Now the Virgin will come and the Golden Age return.)

They approach the manger and their language within each stanza
traverses all the range of dignity, reverence, witty prattling with a
human child, and tenderness before an infant God:

> Haylle, lytlle tyne mop, rewarder of mede,
> Haylle, bot oone drop of grace at my nede,
> Haylle lytlle mylk sop, Haylle David Sede,
> Of our crede thou art crop, haylle, in God hede.
>   This balle
> That thou wold resave [receive]
> Lytylle is that I have,
> This wylle I vowche save
>   To play thee with alle,

while the third shepherd expresses in his exclamations the full witty
mystery of a helpless Almighty, an infant Godhead:

> Haylle, maker of man, haylle, swetyng,
> Haylle, so as I can, haylle, praty mytyng.

This union of tenderness with sophisticated wit is one characteristic medieval manner; *Secunda Pastorum* carries it forward in
another mode. This play also opens with a plaint on man's
destitution:

> No wonder as it standys if we be poore,
> For the tylthe of our landys lyys falow as the floore.

But after this opening lament the shepherds are joined by a fictional character, Mak, a thieving liar who practises witchcraft. He steals a lamb from them and they visit his house in search of it, to be told that a baby lies sick in the cradle. The shepherds peer in and find the 'baby', the stolen lamb, to be remarkable:

> What the dewill is this? He has a long snowte!

They take Mak out and toss him in a blanket before proceeding to the manger to worship the Holy Child. This is manifestly no capricious 'comic interlude' between two scenes of gravity. Mak is certainly a proper representative of fallen mankind; in the lamb in the cradle there are hints of the sheep lost and found and an anticipation of the child in the manger who is the Lamb of God. There is satiric laughter here and boisterous buffoonery but it does no more than strengthen the adoration and the compassion in the final scene in which the worship is as tender and as complex in mood as that of *Prima Pastorum*:

> Hayll, comly and clene! hayll yong child!
> Hayll, Maker, as I meyne, of a madyn so mylde!
> ... Have a bob of cherys! [cherries]

And over all there is the certainty of serene truth announced by the angel:

> God is made your freynd now at this morne.

Man's nature then is explored in its grotesquerie and tenderness, in its crude grossness and its comic potentiality. We are here perhaps nearest to the temper which produced the confounding insights of medieval carving and stained glass: the comic, obscene and blasphemous images within range of and indeed on occasion confronting the sanctuary itself. A passage in William Golding's *The Spire* (London, 1964) places this quality of the grotesque with complete accuracy:

When he walked towards the west front now, he saw that the gargoyles had respite and waited motionless with straining mouths for what might come next. He would stand, thinking with what accuracy and inspiration those giants had built this place, because the gargoyles seemed cast out of the stone, burst out of the stone like boils or pimples, purging the body of sickness, ensuring by their self-damnation the purity of the whole. Now that the rain had gone, he could see the moss and lichens of green and black, so that some of the gargoyles seemed diseased, as they yelled their soundless blasphemies and derisions into the wind, yet made no more noise than death in another country.

(p. 67)

This is the 'comic mode' of Hieronymus Bosch, of the misericord corbels and glass panels which depict greed, malice and envy at the elbow of grace, of Breughel's *Adoration of the Magi* in which cupidity transfigures the senile faces at the very moment when they offer gifts to the infant Christ. It is a mordant vision, straining comedy to breaking-point; indeed the 'comedy of evil' at the centre of religious art can compass human sin and the devils themselves, as we find in the irony of the Cornish *Ordinalia*, a medieval cycle in Cornish.

Beelzebub and Satan make ready for Abel's despatch to hell:

> Dun ganso the dre warnot
>   th'again arluth Lucifer
> My a gan an conternot
>   he ty dyscant ym-kener.
> (Bring him quickly to our Lord Lucifer;
> I shall sing the melody and you shall sing the descant.)

Here the anticipation of a Faustian scene is given comic irony not simply by the song of the devils but by their parody of the terms of liturgical music as an accompaniment to the descent into hell.

Marlowe's *Faustus* is a very precise test of this intensifying function of comedy, its ability both to crystallize our perception of a tragic scene and to lead us to see ironies within it. The text is course teasing and it is difficult to know the extent of Marlowe's own hand especially in the comic scenes in question; this textual problem, however, need not in fact trouble the reader or the play-goer, for, while certain of the farcical scenes may not be to our contemporary taste, many of the scenes of apparently pure inter-polated comedy (whether by Marlowe or a later hand) in fact comment on the main action like an ironic chorus. Two moments in the play may be contrasted: the first concerns Faustus's signing of his pact with the devil; we may sympathize with the scholar's desire to compass all knowledge, even that included under the ban of 'curiosity'; what strikes the reader as depraved levity is the manner and temper of his inordinate desire, his final signing away of his soul with the concluding words of Christ on the cross:

> Consummatum est: this bill is ended
> And Faustus hath bequeathed his soul to Lucifer.

By contrast with this deliberate self-damnation while using words of grace, we may compare the 'comedy' of Wagner and 'Clown'. Wagner says that the buffoon is so hungry 'that I know he would give his soul to the devil for a shoulder of mutton, though it were blood-raw.' The Clown protests that (unlike Faustus, as we may remark) he would need a better bargain for an immortal soul:

> How! My soul to the devil for a shoulder of mutton, though 't were blood-raw? Not so, good friend: by'r lady, I had need for it well roasted, and good sauce to it, if I pay so dear.

Comedy here performs its characteristic choric function; out of the mouth of a simpleton the essential triviality of the learned Faustus's sin is brought in focus; in later and even more complex plays this subtle variant of 'comic relief' is developed yet further.

Macbeth contains the most frequently cited instance, the short scene of the porter at the moment of tragic tension of Duncan's murder. Though his full appearance (Act II, Scene iii) comprises

less than four hundred words, it has been as much a virtuoso piece
for a 'character actor' as that of the first grave-digger in *Hamlet* –
and its setting is more immediately tragic. Macbeth has killed
Duncan; he has listened with the certainty of damnation to the
drunken pieties of the grooms ('I had most need of blessing and
"Amen" stuck in my throat') while he contemplates the 'filthy
witness' of the blood on his hands. The latter phrase is his wife'
and as she utters the words of ironic anticipation,

A little water cleans us of this deed

(for she was to know before her death that that cleansing could no
be accomplished by 'all the perfume of Arabia'), the knocking
begins at the gate. The immediate prelude to the porter's entrance
is Macbeth's pathetic plea:

Wake Duncan with thy knocking! I would thou couldst!

and the porter responds, immediately, with a wry prefiguring
the truth about Dunsinane:

Here's knocking indeed! If a man were porter of hell-gate, he shou
have old turning the key.

And his speech closes with a bitter confirmation of its opening:

But this place is too cold for hell. I'll devil-porter it no longer.

Despite its comedy (and few actors of the scene have felt able
resist the temptation to 'play it for laughs'), the porter's lo
speech carries the clearest exposition of a central abstract theme
the play, that of equivocation. The play begins with a dubio
riddle, 'fair is foul and foul is fair'. It continues with ambiguo
prognostications of a fortune which 'cannot be ill, cannot be goo
and ends with the revelation that all prophecies and all fortu
have been the equivocal cheatings of improper aspiration: a wo
does proceed from one place to another apparently against nat

and Macbeth is defeated by one 'not of woman born'. At the heart of these equivocations lies the porter's definition of an equivocator 'that could swear in both the scales against either scale' and he proceeds to a ribald examination of the 'equivocation of drink'. In this respect he belongs with those other bitter amateur fools, Cleopatra's asp-seller and Hamlet's grave-digger, who express unpalatable truths in jesting words.

And they all belong with the professional fools, with Lear's court-jester, with Feste and Touchstone, and with Thersites who, without licence, sets himself up in their number. Touchstone, despite certain implications in his name, is no infallible commentator on affairs and conspicuously fails to modify experience acquired in courtly circles to fit the circumstances of rural life in the Forest of Arden. But Feste, so tuneful and apparently carefree, is the just choric centre of *Twelfth Night*. Urbane, with a touch of condescension towards Sir Andrew and Sir Toby ('one of thy kin has a most weak pia mater'), he is sharply acrid in his understanding of Orsino and direct in his judgement. After singing 'Come away, death' before the Duke he takes quick offence at a suggestion of payment and takes his leave of Orsino in shrewd terms:

Now the melancholy god protect thee; and the tailor make thy doublet of changeable taffeta, for thy mind is a very opal. I would have men of such constancy put to sea, that their business might be everything and their intent everywhere.

(II. iv.)

This effrontery of comment, so accurately formulating Orsino's weakness, passes beyond the brief of a mere 'licensed jester' and is a pretaste of the exchange between Lear and his fool.

Fool How now nuncle! Would I had two coxcombs and two daughters!
Lear Why, my boy?
Fool If I gave them all my living, I'd keep my coxcombs myself. There's mine; beg another of thy daughters.

    Lear Take heed, sirrah – the whip
    Fool Truth's a dog must to kennel; he must be whipp'd out, when my
    Lady the brach may stand by th' fire and stink.

(I. iv.)

Yet the fool is undeterred in his truth-telling, involving Kent in
the attempt to force Lear to see the truth of his bereft condition:

    Lear Dost thou call me fool, boy?
    Fool All thy other titles thou hast given away; that thou wast born
    with.
    Kent This is not altogether fool, my lord.
    Fool No faith, lords and great men will not let me; if I had a monopoly
    out, they would have part on 't.

(I. iv.)

Feste and Lear's Fool raise sharply once more the close relation
between the tragic and comic vision; indeed, there are dramatic
structures within which it is profoundly difficult to distinguish the
modes, most notably *Troilus and Cressida*. This play occupies a
kind of limbo in the *First Folio* of 1623 between the histories and
tragedies. Though itself called in its folio title *The Tragedy of
Troilus and Cressida*, in the two quartos of 1609 it is successively
The Historie and *The Famous Historie of Troylus and
Cresseid*; while the 'Epistle to the Reader' contains the remarkable
words:

    So much and such savored salt of witte is in his Commedies, that they
    seeme (for their height of pleasure) to be borne in that sea that brought
    forth *Venus*: Amongst all there is none more witty than this: And had
    I time I would comment upon it . . . It deserves such a labour, as well
    as the best Comedy in *Terence* or *Plautus*

Out of this confusion of *genres* has been born both the desire to
place it in its own category of Jonsonian 'comicall satyre', and the
quality of witty comment by its 'fool'. Thersites has a penetrating
savagery which puts him on the further side of satire even from
Lear's 'bitter Fool'. The clarity of his analysis of political and social

morals is of the same order as that of Feste or the fool in *Lear*, though expressed in vituperative language unlike anything else in Shakespearian comedy. After having observed the military leaders quite early in the play (in Act 2, scene 3), he concludes:

> Here is such patchery, such juggling, and such knavery. All the argument is a whore and a cuckold – a good quarrel to draw emulous faction and bleed to death upon. Now the dry serpigo on the subject, and war and lechery confound all!

By the middle of the play this 'fool' is satirically undermining even the moral basis of his own judgements:

> A plague of opinion! A man may wear it on both sides, like a leather jerkin,

but by the end of the play (Act 5, scene 2) it is left to Thersites to make the choric comment, identical in tone with that with which he began:

> Lechery, lechery! Still wars and lechery! Nothing else holds fashion. A burning devil take them!

No other general category than comedy will compass this perplexing play and it is doubly ironic that the moral centrality of the play is maintained not so much by the sententious Ulysses, with his main plea for social order and 'degree', as by the agonized condemnation of this moral and physical outcast, Thersites. Witty, even scurrilous comment on the follies (and crimes) of man is certainly a prime function of comedy but in this play the critical vision has been carried to the point where the very fabric of comedy, its poised tone, is threatened. Little wonder that one of the most distinguished commentators on our classical drama, Miss Una Ellis-Fermor, should have described this play in terms which would not normally be regarded as appropriate to comedy:

> The dark night of the soul comes down upon the unilluminated wreckage of the universe of vision. The play of *Troilus and Cressida*

> remains as one of the few living and unified expressions of this
> experience . . . The idea of chaos, of disjunction, of ultimate formless-
> ness and negation, has by a supreme act of artistic mastery been given
> form.
>
> (*Frontiers of Drama*, p. 72)

Chaos, the denial of the supreme virtues and values, of love
steadfastness, lawful order and chivalry, these are the centra
ingredients of a play which staggers to the verge of forma
tragedy; if Thersites may be numbered with the porter, th
countryman, the grave-digger and the fool of Shakespearia
tragedy (while remaining in some sort 'cousin german' to Fest
and Touchstone) then a strange and disquieting dramatic art ha
made of him the most confounding exemplar of 'comic relief'. T
the Aristophanic analogies of this disquieting mode we mu
return later.

Milton would seem to be a powerful witness against the argu
ment here maintained, that comedy has a peculiar power when see
in relation to tragedy. In a prefatory essay to *Samson Agoniste*
he writes:

> Tragedy, as it was antiently compos'd, hath been ever held the graves
> moralest, and most profitable of all other Poems . . . Heretofore M
> in highest dignity have labour'd not a little to be thought able
> compose a Tragedy.

But, he complains, the tragic form has been tainted by associati
with unworthy material:

> This is mention'd to vindicate Tragedy from the small esteem,
> rather infamy, which in the account of many it undergoes at this d
> with other common Interludes; hap'ning through the Poets error
> intermixing Comic stuff with Tragic sadness and gravity; or introdu
> ing trivial and vulgar persons, which by all judicious hath
> counted absurd.

Among the injudicious, by Milton's reckoning, must be counted Sophocles, Euripides and Shakespeare, less concerned for the purity of genres than for the powerful presentation of emotional and intellectual antitheses. And in our own theatre T. S. Eliot has explored this relationship with an irony of especial force. In *Murder in the Cathedral* the instrument of ironic comment is found in two forms, focusing the tragic issue. Immediately before the murder Thomas stills the fears of his priests:

> No life here is sought for but mine,
> And I am not in danger: only near to death.

> (p. 67)

Whether the closing words of that declaration are recognized as irony will, of course, depend on the credal assumptions of the listener; but the comic irony is quite unambiguous in the speeches of the knights after the murder:

> When you come to the point, it does go against the grain to kill an Archbishop, especially when you have been brought up in good Church traditions ... I may say that I have never known a man so well qualified for the highest rank of the Civil Service.

> (p. 76)

By including a quite extended scene of naturalistic serio-comic comment by the knights Eliot takes great risks with the integrity of the play's tone, the risk that all tragic writers take in 'intermixing Comic stuff with Tragic sadness and gravity'; for their purposes at this point are complex beyond Milton's imagining. And it is of course no matter of contrived art alone that weds the two kinds of mutual comment. In a broadcast talk (printed in *The Listener* on 9 October 1958) Mr Enoch Powell recounts the historic facts which preceded Becket's murder:

> Then, with his cross still in his hands [Becket] made for the door, and before anyone could stop him, had passed out again into the great hall, where, in his haste, he tripped over a bundle of firewood and

barely avoided falling. Through the crowd and the jeering he got to the doorway and on to his horse, but in the throng outside, one of his Chaplains could not reach his own mount and so got up behind the Archbishop. Then came another hitch: the castle gate was locked and the porter engaged in a private scuffle with someone ... So the Archbishop, 'with some difficulty', as the narrative goes, 'managing his horse, holding his cross and blessing the crowd', made his way back to his lodging at St. Andrew's. Before the following dawn he had left Northampton with three companions and within a fortnight made his way to France and began the exile from which he returned only to martyrdom.

Mr Enoch Powell makes a just comment on that remarkable passage and shifts the historical fact into the orbit of dramatic art, with its ironic intersection of modes:

> The authenticity of the details is unmistakable; we see the recognisable types of human behaviour; the strange mixture of histrionics and heroism in the Archbishop, the interplay of comedy and tragedy, homely incident and grand drama, within the setting of the insoluble conflict.

It may be nice discrimination which decides whether life imitated art (as Oscar Wilde declared) or art held the mirror up to nature it is quite certain that whether in life or art, whether in the historic conflict between a 'real' Becket and a 'real' Henry or in the compressed and formulated art of Eliot, the comic incongruities of human failings and absurdities are seen to accompany the height and depths of tragic action. A saint may stumble over firewood and fumble vainly with his crozier on the way to martyrdom - and, having died, be seen by the impercipient to be 'well-qualified for the highest rank of the Civil Service'. For this mixture of the noble and the ridiculous, the comic, sublime and tragic, is characteristic of the very nature of man. For a blind man, tentatively winning his sight, saw men 'as trees walking'; in the tragic universe of Lear, man is a 'forked radish'; to Hamlet, this 'paragon of animals' is 'the quintessence of dust'; and at the end of things the valorous Hotspur is 'food for worms'. It may well be that the apparent conclusion of this initial argument has some validity: that the comic vision penetrates the secret of man's condition best when it is seen in relation to the structure of tragic art. Indeed, within the pattern of one play an identical insight may issue from very different moods and settings; after the killing of Polonius the flyting 'madness' of Hamlet declares that

> We fat all creatures else to fat us, and we fat ourselves for maggots; your fat king and your lean beggar is but variable service – two dishes but to one table; that's the end.
>
> (IV. iii.)

Only a scene or two later, the 'philosophy' of the gravedigger and the finding of the jester Yorick's skull lead him to the same conclusion:

> Where be your gibes now, your gambols, your songs, your flashes of merriment, that were wont to set the table on a roar? Not one now, to mock your own grinning? Quite chap-fallen? Now get up to my lady's chamber, and tell her, let her paint an inch thick, to this favour she must come; make her laugh at that.
>
> (V. i.)

Each of these scenes, of predominant gravity, stimulates the audience to moments of laughter; and both tragedy and levity are part of the same vision, of the bizarre *danse macabre* in which lady and jester, king and lean beggar dance together to the same end.

5
Comical-Satire and 'Tragi-Comedy'

'The actors are come hither, my lord . . . the best actors in the world either for tragedy, comedy, history, pastoral, pastoral-comical, historical-pastoral, tragical-historical, tragical-comical – historical-pastoral, scene individable, or poem unlimited. Seneca cannot be too heavy, nor Plautus too light.'

(*Hamlet*, II. ii.)

Entia non sint multiplicanda praeter necessitas is a good philosophic maxim, an excellent principle of literary criticism: kinds, categories, genres should not proliferate in order to tidy up our muddy thinking. Yet our argument in the previous section embarrassingly pushed comedy to breaking-point and it was not surprising, in a self-conscious literary age, that, in order to save a semblance of the classical orders, the genera should have been subdivided into species, if not quite to the extent suggested grotesquely by Polonius. The compromise between the two great forms of drama is of course found early: Plautus wrote of 'tragico-comoedia' and this is echoed by theorists in the sixteenth century, in Florio's 'tragi-comedia' and, with derogatory overtones, in Sidney's *Apology*, when he denies that true dramatic 'sportfulness' is to be obtained by 'mungrell Tragi-comedie'. In 1603 Samuel Harsnet is more historical in attributing the contemporary mixed mode to its classical analogue: '*Our Daemonopoiia* or *Devill-fiction* is Tragico-Comoedia, a mixture of both as Amphitryo in Plautus is'; while Drummond of Hawthornden, Ben Jonson's friend, is in a very central moralistic tradition in speaking of 'this tragi-comedy, called life'.

All this word-play is an attempt to reconcile forms of behaviour dramatic philosophies, that are instinctively felt to be opposites, irreconcilable. The standard dictionary definitions hesitate between two possibilities when defining tragi-comedy: the *O.E.D.* allows us to choose between 'a play combining the qualities of a tragedy and a comedy' and 'a play mainly of a tragic character but with a happy ending', two very different possibilities, whatever allowances we make for the fact that the brevity of a dictionary definition of necessity begs many questions. We have perhaps hints of the two possibilities when on the one hand Burke writes of the French Revolution in 1790:

> This monstrous tragi-comick scene . . . alternate laughter and tears; alternate scorn and horror,

and on the other hand Macaulay writes in 1849 of

> the plot of the noble tragi-comedy of *Measure for Measure.*

Burke finds in the events of the Revolution a complex alternation of comedy and tragedy, of satire and reprehension; Macaulay on the other hand (by the weighting of the adjective 'noble') makes of tragi-comedy not the 'mungrell' offspring of nobler parents which Sidney deplored, but a kind in itself which contributed towards elucidating Shakespeare's 'dark comedy', *Measure for Measure.*

It is particularly interesting that Philippe Quinault (1635–88), an undistinguished but highly 'professional' writer (he collaborated with Molière, writing lyrics for *Psyché*, and with Lully, preparing libretti for his operas) should have formulated with some finality for the French theatre of the seventeenth century, the nature of the dramatic categories its theorists were intent on maintaining in their purity. His play *La Comédie sans Comédie* was produced in 1654 and carries very far the characteristic comic insight of the superimposition of the world of play and the world of theatre, the identity of actor and role. For some of the names of the characters in this play are the actual names of the actors themselves, while its structure, intent to demonstrate that 'all the world's a stage', is highly theoretic in its implications. The first act records the attempt of the actors Hauteroche and La Roque to impress the mercenary La Fleur with the significance of their craft. La Roque describes the motives which move him:

> Je me suis vu souvent un sceptre entre les mains,
> Dans un rang au-dessus du reste des humains;
> J'ai de mille Héros réglé les destinées,
> J'ai vu dessous mes pieds des Têtes couronnées,
> Et j'ai par des exploits aussi fameux que grands,
> Vengé les justes Rois & détruit les tyrans;
> J'ai conquis des trésors, j'ai forcé des murailles,
> J'ai donné des combats, j'ai gagné des batailles,
> Et me suis vu vingt fois possesseur glorieux
> De tout ce que la terre a de plus précieux.
>
> (Often have I held a sceptre in my hands and occupied
> a rank above all other men. I have settled the fate of
> a thousand champions, seen crowned heads grovel at
> my feet, avenged good kings and undone tyrants by
> means of exploits as famous as they are great. I have
> conquered treasures, breached walls, fought and won
> battles and been proud possessor, twenty times over,
> of all the precious things the earth contains.)

La Fleur is impressed by this comically dubious rhetoric bu wishes to know the vocation which the young men follow. They give the abashed answer 'La Comédie', a way of life wholly con temptible in the merchant's view:

> La Comédie! Hé quoi? ce sont là vos grands biens?
> Vous n'êtes donc, Messieurs, que des Comédiens.
> [Comedy! What! those are your great means?
> You are nothing, sirs, but actors.]

This attack on their profession spurs the company to a fu demonstration of skill and each succeeding act is a complete genr in a significant order: *Pastorale, Comédie, Tragédie, Tragi-Comédie (En Machines)*. This mechanical *tour-de-force* at once uniting and maintaining the disparateness of the genres, yet calls upon tragi-comedy as a final reconciling form, to which even the churlish La Fleur must concede:

> Votre Art dans ces effais m'a paru noble & doux.

It is a far cry from this echo of stringent classical theory to the subtler reflection in Macaulay's phrase, 'the noble tragi-comedy of *Measure for Measure*'. But after all both blunt and sophisticated dramatists and critics, in treating tragi-comedy, are manipulating a category with a consistent history of critical usage. This is not the case with associated attempts to find adequate terms for other plays which appear to strain comedy to its limits; *Measure for Measure*, already defined in complex terms, stands, with *All's Well, Hamlet* and *Troilus and Cressida* as 'Shakespeare's Problem Plays' and, if Ernest Schanzer's argument in his influential book be accepted, *Julius Caesar* and *Antony and Cleopatra* must be added to their number (Schanzer, *Problem Plays of Shakespeare*, London, 1963). It is a measure of our critical insecurity concerning this group that the term 'Problem Plays' or 'Problem Comedies' has been frequently replaced by 'Dark Comedies', which in fact extends the implication to either opacity in interpretation or to a dark, sardonic or even cynical outlook. It is certainly no mere coincidence that those among them which used to be less frequently played have been given more regular and more serious attention in the theatre since the advent of the Theatre of the Absurd, with its dark assumption that it is 'one of the ways of facing up to a universe that has lost its meaning and purpose' (*The Absurd*, p. 11, by A. P. Hinchliffe in this series).

Before these quasi-philosophic assumptions are examined in relation to comic theory, we should place these 'problematic' works in relation to comical satire in the words of Shakespeare's contemporaries; for in these mixed or ambiguous terms, 'dark comedy', 'tragi-comedy', 'comical satire', we return yet again in this study to the profound difficulty of demarcation between the tragic and the comic temper. Indeed, the group of plays by Ben Jonson to which the term 'comical satire' has been consistently applied since his own day (*Every Man Out of his Humour, Cynthia's Revels* and *The Poetaster*) pose especially difficult problems in assessing their peculiar tone of voice and even their satiric intention. Nor is this difficulty confined to the works of Ben Jonson in this 'comic' mode; his immediate predecessor Marlowe, in *The Jew of Malta*, and his contemporary Webster, confront us with a like ambiguity of temper. The tone of the former was nicely judged in the famous passage in an early essay by T. S. Eliot on 'Christopher Marlowe' (reprinted from *The Sacred Wood*, 1920, in *Selected Essays*, 1932):

> If one takes the *Jew of Malta* not as a tragedy, or as a 'tragedy of blood', but as a farce, the concluding act becomes intelligible; and if we attend with a careful ear to the versification, we find that Marlowe develops a tone to suit this farce, and even perhaps that this tone is his most powerful and mature tone. I say farce, but with the enfeebled humour of our times the word is a misnomer; it is the farce of the old English humour, the terribly serious, even savage comic humour, the humour which spent its last breath in the decadent genius of Dickens

We have seen something of this savage grotesquerie of medieval comedy (a bitter glee which Shakespeare extends in certain facets of his Richard III) and have been able to estimate the difficulty of knowing when this dramatic mood veers to satire, sardonic wit, or the comedy of compassion, which sees in a stolen lamb, cradled at a cottage hearth, the prefiguring of a Lamb in a Manger. T. S. Eliot, in another medium than critical prose, identifies this sardonic serio-comic mode in Webster. In his early poem 'Whisper of Immortality' (*Poems*, 1920) he gives a mordant summary of the characteristic attitudes of John Webster's revenge plays:

> Webster was much possessed by death
> And saw the skull beneath the skin;
> And breastless creatures under ground
> Leaned backward with a lipless grin.

And in a later stanza, in which Donne's insights are invoked, even the wry comedy of the 'lipless grin' is excluded for

> He knew the anguish of the marrow
> The ague of the skeleton.

Ben Jonson (like Donne) was capable of giving powerful emotional force to perceptions which were essentially intellectual; in his many pronouncements on the nature of comedy, and his own practice of the art in particular, we sense under the reasonable clarity of the overt statement a considerable pressure of feeling. It is quite startling to catch this undertone in his prologue to *The Alchemist*:

> Our *Scene* is *London* . . .
> Whose manners, now call'd humours, feed the stage:
> And which have still beene subject, for the rage
> Or spleene of *comick*-writers.

Savage indignation' is the appropriate tone for certain kinds of satire in the classical tradition; 'rage' and 'spleen' have rarely been the motive-force of comedy or 'comic-writers' in the English tradition. But in the opening decades of the seventeenth century, poetry and drama, without perhaps reaching very frequently the later, acrid tone of Swift, yet show a violence of feeling which again stretches comedy almost to breaking-point. In his study of *Jacobean City Comedy* (London, 1968) Dr Brian Gibbons explores some of the areas in which poetic satire – Donne's in particular – shares its tone with the 'comical-satire' we are here considering. The voice has a bitter edge, whether, in Donne's 'Satire III', the anger is directed towards certain religious follies (in a highly ambivalent line):

> Kinde pitty chokes my spleene;

or, in the savage humour of Jonson's plays, the dramatist has adopted 'a persona of disgust with social and moral corruption and folly' which Dr Gibbons here relates to the 'traditional invective of the medieval Church' (p. 25). In considering the greater complexity of Donne's satires, the conjunction of terms is suggestive:

> Donne's satiric persona has a distinct effect on the response of the readers . . . it establishes a distance between reader and subject, invites astringent, intelligent glee or disgust rather than sympathetic identification with character, scene and experience.
>
> (p. 66)

This is very justly said and corresponds both to our analytical experience of Jonson in the study and to our sense of profound ambiguities of response in the theatre. For though 'astringent, intelligent glee' is far removed from 'disgust', yet in both Donne's satiric poetry and in Jonson's greatest comedies they most disturbingly co-exist. Mr. A. E. Dyson, in a study of Fielding ('Satiric and Comic Theory in relation to Fielding', *Modern Language Quarterly* xviii, 1957) has suggested a definition which further deepens the complexity of this tone we are considering in the Jacobean; for Dyson suggests that satire judges man against an ideal, while comedy sets him against a norm. This proposes a fundamental distinction, for an ideal is by its nature difficult of realization by fallible man, while a norm is humanity's resting point. The two modes then of satire and comedy would seem to oppose bitter glee and compassionate laughter, destructive judgement and an urbane certainty of redemption (as in the insight of Yeats that 'all joyous and creative life is a re-birth as something not oneself' – a compassionate identification which we experience in some measure as we watch true comedy). And yet these two distinct modes of creative experience, of astringent satire and sympathetic comedy, Jonson appears capable of uniting in the highest reaches of his plays – as we find in the conclusion of *The Alchemist* in which savagely dismissive judgement is seen side by side with a casual grace in forgiving some of the gulls; for rage and spleen do not wholly exclude insight into frailty and a generous compassion.

The Jacobean writer's ability to move between the contrasted moods of satire, comedy and tragedy is found in unexpected places. Tourneur's *Revenger's Tragedy* has for most readers been adequately placed by Eliot's comprehensive judgement that the play constitutes 'an intense and unique and horrible vision of life'; yet its latest editor, Professor L. J. Ross (in the Regents Renaissance Drama Series, 1966) suggests a different assessment, in a perspective which makes it very relevant to our present concern:

> The leveling and macabre ironies of the *memento mori* and the Dance of Death . . . wherein Death, the reality of the skull beneath the skin, mocks the worldly blinded by temporal vanities, have been felt to be influential in the play's central symbol, the skull . . . Finally, much of the medieval comic spirit plainly survives in the play's self-conscious burlesque, parodic ironies, antic energy, and grotesque exaggeration.
> (p. xxii)

It is in this temper of bizarre comedy that Vindice, the central avenging character of the play, concludes his address to a skull:

> Be merry, merry;
> Advance thee, O thou terror to fat folks,
> To have their costly three-pil'd flesh worn off
> As bare as this.

It is this temper which Professor Irving Ribner finds in its companion piece, *The Atheist's Tragedy* (The Revels Plays, 1964 – probably unique in its age for its manner of combining seemingly incongruous elements':

> It is rich in comedy of different kinds. The preoccupation with death and sexuality, combined with the most ludicrous of situations, gives to the graveyard scene (IV. iii.) a gothic quality we find in no other

play ... *The Atheist's Tragedy* might have been a dull and insipid morality play, but it is rescued from this fate by the extraordinary (if somewhat macabre) sense of humour which is one of Tourneur's surest qualities.

(p. lvi)

This present essay has been much preoccupied with the power and status of comedy when it is set in a predominantly tragic context; this appears to reach its logical end in the genre which Jonson fashioned, 'comical satire' with its despairing and tragic implications in the plays of his contemporaries. We may test this assumption against an unambiguous if ironic comedy by Chapman, in general a writer more notable for tragedy than comedy. His play *The Widow's Tears* is unjustly neglected, and it has the immediate advantage for our purpose of handling an ancient satiric theme, that of the Widow of Ephesus. It may be revealing to look at this story from Petronius as it was handled by three very different writers, by Chapman, by Christopher Fry and by a sardonic Welsh priest in the Middle Ages. Rarely has a simple tale received such diverse, though consistently 'comic' treatment.

The story in Petronius is an ironic comment on the frailty of human vows and especially of constancy. A widow of Ephesus declares her determination to be enclosed in the grave-vault of her dead husband, and there to die. Outside the graveyard hang executed robbers guarded by a soldier, who sees the light in the tomb, finds the widow and woos her. After three days of love the soldier finds one of the executed thieves removed and he meditates suicide; but the widow redeems his dereliction of duty by causing her own husband's body to be hanged on the robber's cross. Chapman greatly expands this narrative in *The Widow's Tears* and Dr E. M. Smeak, editor in the Regents Series (1966) says of it:

Peter Ure points out that Chapman has turned Petronius' anecdote into 'a full-dress Elizabethan comedy of manners with disguise, resurrection, male jealousy and female wit, and a quite fresh narrative pattern' [*Durham University Journal*, December 1956]. The whole affair hinges upon Lysander's feigned death to test his wife; the irony inherent in Petronius is increased in Chapman's play, for Cynthia mourns over an empty coffin. Further it is the husband, disguised as a soldier, who tempts and wins his own wife, thus ironically proving that the widow's tears are false, even as he becomes his own cuckold ... Chapman's ironic contrasts and foreshadowings have actually increased the comic potential of Petronius' story.

(p. xvii)

Christopher Fry in *A Phoenix Too Frequent* (1946) has given the story (which 'was got from Jeremy Taylor who had it from Petronius') a further comic dimension. His is of course a very amusing play, treating Roman discipline with easy irony:

> Where is the punctual eye
> And where is the cautious voice which made
> Balance-sheets sound like Homer and Homer sound
> Like balance-sheets? The precision of limbs, the amiable
> Laugh, the exact festivity?

(p. 5)

But the issue has a deeper comic irony. Dyamene swiftly loves the young officer and proposes the solution first told in Petronius; but this is with a difference, for behind the laughter and the momentary ironies lies the delicate suggestion of a 'resurrection'. Pressed too far this becomes a ludicrous over-statement; held within the fragility of the closing speeches it carries sufficient gravity to intensify the comedy:

Tegeus   Hang your husband?
  Dynamene, it's terrible, horrible.
Dynamene How little you can understand. I loved
  His life not his death. And now we can give his death
  The power of life. Not horrible: wonderful!
  Isn't it so? That I should be able to feel
  He moves again in the world, accomplishing
  Our welfare. It's more than my grief could do.

(p. 42–3)

This is a delicately poised tone, handling the source material with a quite different irony from Chapman's. But to explore still further the ambiguous possibilities of the comedy in the story from Petronius we may return some centuries to a fourteenth-century Welsh manuscript, *Llyfr Coch Hergest* from which we take the tenth tale in the familiar medieval sequence, 'The Tales of the Seven Sages of Rome'. For more than half its course this story follows the narrative we have examined from Petronius to Fry. But then the plot takes a strangely sardonic turn which is intensified by the mannered formality of the medieval Welsh (which I have tried, with some difficulty, to echo here in a revision of a broadcast in the Third Programme of the B.B.C. in 1952). The widow repeats the familiar suggestions:

'If you gave me your word that you would marry me, I should rid you of this trouble.'
'I give you my word that I shall marry you.'
'This is what you must do,' said she. 'Uncover the man here and hang him in place of the criminal'.

The knight is reluctant and his fastidiousness grows as the widow suggests means to obscure the difference between her husband and the hanged men. The closing passage of the tale in this Welsh version is wholly unlike any of its parallel versions:

'Yet what is the use of that?' said the knight: 'the criminal was toothless.'
'I shall make this one toothless,' said she; and taking a boulder she struck him until his mouth and teeth were smashed by the force of the blow.
'Yes,' said the knight, 'but the outlaw was bald.'
'I shall make this one bald,' said she, and took her husband's head between her knees; no woman shearing nor man shaving was swifter than she as she stripped her husband's head; soon from forehead to crown she left no hair unplucked, any more than a parchment-maker on a parchment skin; and when she had done she told the knight to hang him.

'By my faith, I shall not hang him, nor shall you; and if you were the only woman in the world I would not have you; for if you are as unfaithful as this to the husband who married you when you were a maid and who took his life for love of you, how unfaithful will you be to me, whom you never saw until tonight! Therefore go your way, for I shall never have you.'

This is an instructive group of narratives and may serve as a parable illustrating the prevailing argument we have hitherto pursued, that within any situation loosely definable as 'comic' there exist possibilities of profound latent differences, of sardonic comment on human frailty, of ironic, even destructive wit, of compassionate involvement in the pathos of vulnerable human concerns, and finally of a recognition that the comic mask sometimes leers with a grimace dangerously near the tragic. Samuel Johnson has expressed this complexity of mode more nobly than any other critic when he explores Shakespeare's practice in 'mingled drama':

Shakespeare's plays are not in the rigorous and critical sense either tragedies or comedies, but compositions of a distinct kind; exhibiting the real state of sublunary nature, which partakes of good and evil, joy and sorrow, mingled with endless variety of proportion and innumerable modes of combination; and expressing the course of the world, in which the loss of one is the gain of another; in which, at the same time, the reveller is hasting to his wine, and the mourner burying his friend; in which the malignity of one is sometimes defeated by the frolic of another; and many mischiefs and many benefits are done and hindered without design.

(Wimsatt, W. K., *Dr Johnson on Shakespeare*,
Penguin Shakespeare Library, 1969, p. 22)

With this characteristic Johnsonian measure and wisdom in criticism we have reached a convenient halting-point in our exploration of comic modes of writing. There have been moments when the comic spirit has invaded a work of prevailing tragic insight, or, conversely, when a glimpse of tragedy has darkened a work of prevailing radiant gaiety, when the demarcation of tragedy and comedy has seemed none too easy to define; when indeed, to consider the genre with which we are most immediately concerned, comedy has seemed to reach its greatest stature not in independence but in association with the darker insights of tragedy. Samuel Johnson has again something to say in pursuing this fruitful confusion. Writing of the *First Folio* of 1623 he says:

> The players [Heminge and Condell, Shakespeare's fellows] who in their edition divided our author's works into comedies, histories, and tragedies, seem not to have distinguished the three kinds by any very exact or definite ideas.

Thus Shakespeare wrote in an age in which the ending or 'catastrophe' denominated the nature of the work:

> An action which ended happily to the principal persons, *however serious or distressful through its intermediate incidents*, in their opinion constituted a comedy.

Johnson's rider to this statement brings us very near the variety of mood which we have seen to be latent in such a theme as 'The Widow of Ephesus':

> ... And plays were written which, by changing the catastrophe, were tragedies today and comedies tomorrow.

Tragedy was quite logically comedy's converse:

> Tragedy was not in those times a poem of more general dignity or elevation than comedy; it required only a calamitous conclusion, with which the common criticism of that age was satisfied, whatever lighter pleasure it afforded in its progress.

These judgements were written by Samuel Johnson in 1765 in the Preface to his edition of *Shakespeare's Plays*. His dictum that 'plays were written which, by changing the catastrophe, were tragedies today and comedies tomorrow' was remarkably echoed in France a decade later. Beaumarchais' *The Barber of Seville* was first performed in February 1775 and, in his *Lettre Modérée sur la chute et la critique du Barbier de Séville*, he writes concerning genre in drama, defending his work against the rigidity of neo-classical criticism:

> Un vieillard amoureux prétend épouser demain sa pupille; un jeune amant plus adroit le prévient, et ce jour même en fait sa femme à la barbe et dans la maison du tuteur. Voilà le fond, dont on eût pu faire, avec un égal succès, une tragédie, une comédie, un drame, un opéra *et caetera*. L'*Avare* de Molière est-il autre chose? *Le Grand Mithridate* est-il autre chose? Le genre d'une pièce, comme celui de toute autre action, dépend moins du fond des choses que des caractères qui les mettent en oeuvre.

> (An amorous old man intends to marry his Ward on the morrow; a more skilful young rival intervenes and cocks a snook at the guardian by marrying her this very day in the guardian's own house. This is the basic material from which one could equally easily have fashioned a tragedy, a comedy, a melodrama (or tragi-comic *drama*), an opera, etc. What more is there to Molière's L'*Avare*? What more is there to *Le Grand Mithridate*? The genre of a play, like that of any activity, depends less on the basic material than on the characters which bring it to life.)

And there for the moment we must allow the matter of genre to rest; in the argument hitherto we have found on the one hand that comedy is profoundly difficult to define in the abstract and equally difficult to distinguish from other comic modes, the grotesque, the absurd, the ironic and the farcical. But in concrete terms, in particular moments in literature when definition is set aside, the comic is not difficult to detect. Indeed it confronts us with its own especial view of life, its peculiar intensity alongside the intensity of the tragic vision. And in mixed modes, in tragi-comedy or those moments when the radiance or the ironic wit of comedy trans-figures a tragic scene, what do we say of definition? If there are literary works which seem to elude description as tragedy or comedy, we seem for the moment to be provided with two possible 'laboratory tests'. There is first the matter of emotional and intellectual intensity, and to distinguish here between the differing intensity of the tragic or comic mode is a matter of some critical tact and experience. Or, in the second place, we may properly fall back upon the traditional reliance upon the play's ending, and here we may attempt a modest definition of comedy as the permanent possibility of a happy resolution.

Difficulties of course remain. Shakespeare's *Winter's Tale* raises some of the questions quite acutely. If we depend, with Samuel Johnson and a host of other writers in the central critical tradition, on the test of its ending, then it is clearly a comedy; and yet criticism has always stammered over the genre of this play and its fellows, *The Tempest, Cymbeline* and *Pericles*. For some generations they were 'the Romances', an autumnal emergence from Shakespeare's tragic period. Symbolic interpretation enriched their content and parallels with 'parables of losing and finding' gave them an intensity which located their plots at the moment of a narrow escape from tragedy into comedy. Of recent years critics have tended not to prejudice their findings and the four works are known more neutrally as 'The Last Plays', leaving the particularities of each play beyond definition. For it would seem inadequate, for *The Tempest* or *The Winter's Tale*, to confine their definition as comedy to the happy resolution of their concluding scenes. For the core of Prospero's long story is exile on an island; at his return to 'society' he abjures his magic learning and buries his books – a resolution in joy and a reconciliation to the society of former enemies at the same time clearly involves renunciation and a sense of loss. In the companion play, Perdita, who was lost, is found again; the marble-flesh of Hermione is discovered by Leontes with the awe, in his exclamation, 'O, she's warm!' It is a conclusion of radiant reconciliation and this is the stuff of comedy. But there are insistent questions which nag at the memory of the sensitive theatre-goer or reader: what of the dead Mamillius, heir to the throne? or the sixteen-year cloistral exile of Hermione, or Leontes' lone penitence for bitter, tragic jealousy? of the childhood and young adolescence of Perdita, so aptly named? It is not for nothing that the play's temper and notable crises recollect high moments not in earlier comedies but in tragedies; that Perdita, distributing nosegays, so deftly echoes Ophelia in her tragic moments. For as Ophelia distinguishes the young Laertes from the ageing King and Queen:

> There's rosemary that's for remembrance; pray you love, remember...
> There's rue for you ... O, you must wear your rue with a difference,
> (*Hamlet* IV. v.)

so Perdita in her spontaneous joy distinguishes between middle-age and youth:

> Hot lavender, mints, savory, marjoram;
> The marigold, that goes to bed with th' sun
> And with him rises weeping; these are flowers
> Of middle summer, and I think they are given
> To men of middle age ...
>   O Proserpina,
> For the flowers now ...
> Daffodils ... violets ... pale primroses ...
> The crown imperial; lilies of all kinds,
> The flower-de-luce being one: O, these I lack
> To make you garlands of, and my sweet friend
> To strew him o'er and o'er!
> (*The Winter's Tale*, IV. iii.)

At the other end of the emotional scale, the centre and spring of potential tragedy in this play is a jealousy, which in word and action recalls Othello's. For, comedy though this work clearly is, the possibility of tragic waste lies at its centre; it is by a narrow

escape indeed that Leontes avoids parody of Othello and he might
so easily have cried, in face of his many and long deprivations,

> O, the pity of it, Paulina, the pity of it!

So near does the art of comedy steer to the matter of tragedy.

6

The Ritual of Comedy

> It hath been sung at festivals,
> On ember-eves and holy-ales.

When Gower, the chorus-poet of Shakespeare's *Pericles* comes to sing an old song, he guarantees its quality by association with those recurrent rituals of the countryside, the religious and folk festivals and 'ember-days'. During Shakespeare's lifetime these were still a living memory and even the growing towns preserved their ritual patterns of shows, masques and progresses, with royal and other 'entrances' to add pageantry to state occasions. The ritual pattern of comedy, like that of tragedy, was still linked to the annual festival rhythms, whether these were the consciously christian celebrations of birth, death and resurrection, of Christmas, Good Friday and Easter-day, or the mythical archetypes of 'birth, copulation and death' in the rhythms of the natural year: the fecundity of summer, the ripe maturity of autumn, the death and burial of winter and the renewal and birth of spring. There is clearly a related rhythm between the annual pattern of pagan and christian rite: equally clearly comedy echoes this mythic pattern, whether, as we shall see later, it is comedy of the Aristophanic, 'scapegoat' kind, or, with Shakespeare, regularly celebrates the 'green world'. For the twentieth-century reader and critic, this pattern largely lost or defective both in its natural and spiritual forms, has to be self-consciously recreated, a combined exercise of scholarship and imagination which poses its own problems of dramatic interpretation, both in the study and in the theatre.

For criticism, from E. K. Chambers to C. L. Barber by way of

Northrop Frye, has made us richly aware of these fundamental and frequently unconscious sources of comic action. C. L. Barber's essay 'The Saturnalian Pattern in Shakespeare's Comedy' (*Sewanee Review*, Autumn 1951) reminds us of the universality of these patterns:

> *Ulysses* and *The Waste Land* expressed life in a modern city by representing it as recapitulating basic myths and rituals ... Psychology and ethnology have developed a corresponding set of generic names – 'the Oedipus complex', 'the fertility spirit', 'the rebirth archetype'.

and we may perhaps profitably link these current relationships of very diverse disciplines to such classic explorations of 'folk elements' in drama as Chambers' *Medieval Stage*, which reminded us of the rich, largely unconscious tradition on which the creativity of the Elizabethan theatre depended. But Barber reminds us that that tradition requires *conscious* exploration on our part:

> In earlier cultures such patterns were implicit in particular observances and did not need to be named. We have to name them ['the Oedipus complex', 'the fertility spirit', etc. etc.] because for our cosmopolitan and relativistic mentality no particular symbolism is any longer self-evident.

Barber then describes a method by which the attentive reader of sophisticated drama may develop an awareness of more primitive sources and springs of action (and his own *Shakespeare's Festive Comedy* in 1959 amply justified his method):

> To explore patterns which drama has in common with ritual is one way to develop this awareness, to see how the role precedes the character, how the larger rhythm of the whole action shapes and indeed creates the parts.

We may test this briefly for ourselves by contrasting the endings of certain Shakespearian comedies. Northrop Frye has located the 'romantic comedies' of Shakespeare in 'the tradition of the seasonal ritual play' (in his influential essay 'The Mythos of Spring' in *The Anatomy of Criticism*, 1957):

> We may call it the drama of the green world, its plot being assimilated to the ritual theme of the triumph of life and love over the waste land . . . The action of the comedy begins in a world represented as a normal world, moves into the green world, goes into a metamorphosis there in which the comic resolution is achieved, and returns to the normal world.
>
> (p. 182)

He cites as principal examples of this ritual of renewal, *The Two Gentlemen of Verona*, *A Midsummer Night's Dream*, *As You Like It* and *The Merry Wives*, and proceeds to the further comment:

> In *The Merchant of Venice* the second ['green'] world takes the form of Portia's mysterious house in Belmont, with its magic caskets and the wonderful cosmological harmonies that proceed from it in the fifth act.
>
> (p. 182–3)

This is all very justly said and from it we must proceed to distinguish the richer particularities with which Shakespeare concludes his comedies. It is very suggestive here to contrast the methods of *As You Like It*, *The Merry Wives*, *The Dream* and *Love's Labour's Lost* (to put them, for this purpose only, in a logical and not a chronological order) as Shakespeare brings the pattern of each play to its conclusion in a renewed rhythm of life.

As You Like It squares with Frye's account of the issues of 'green-world' comedy, charged 'with the symbolism of the victory of summer over winter', and one of the instruments of this happy resolution is the highly sophisticated dramatic form of a masque. On the page the Masque of Hymen is deceptively brief; elaborated with music, 'entry', dancing 'signifying matrimony' and the gracious involvement of many of the diverse characters in the marriage rite, this masque bulks significantly in the close of the play – and it is highly formal, a courtly ceremony, rather than a primitive ritual, whatever archetypal memories the hymeneal rites recall.

The Merry Wives makes a quite different concluding statement. Falstaff may be a primitive 'lord of misrule'; he may be (again to quote Frye – here pleasantly ironic) a fertility spirit. But the tone of the rites enacted in Windsor Forest smacks pretty certainly of an ironic 'send-up' of the myth of Diana and Actaeon, set here very firmly within the commonplaces of bourgeois comedy.

The Dream is more complex and much subtler. 'Primitive' and 'mythic' it certainly is, and at many levels. The fairy world is given tangible credibility both in its beneficent and darker aspects. But there is a genuine ambiguity concerning the relative placing of the 'green' and 'normal' worlds, concerning the relative values of the 'waking' and the 'dreaming' state. In this play we most profitably look not only at the actual ending of the action itself but at the critical conclusion for Bottom when he wakes from his dream of 'faerie'. It is comic and should properly be played as comedy, but at the core of the scene is the real gravity of his dislocated speech concerning his visionary world:

> The eye of man hath not heard, the ear of man hath not seen, man's hand is not able to taste, his tongue to conceive, nor his heart to report what my dream was.

Editors regularly relate this to a biblical source, St Paul at 1 Corinthians ii, v. 9, 'Eye hath not seen . . . the things which God hath prepared . . .' Much nearer to Bottom's vision and to the sacramental quality in the two phrases 'Man's hand is not able to taste, his tongue to conceive', is the passage in St John's first Epistle:

> That which we have seen with our eyes, which we have looked upon and our hands have handled, of the Word of life.

Bottom has been neither wholly confused nor wholly deceived in his dreaming world. After the marriage rites have been marked by that other dreaming world of his play of Pyramus and Thisbe, he will doubtless return to Athens with refreshment from the wood's 'green world'; it is not fanciful to suppose from this crucial speech that he will return not merely 'refreshed' but with 'something of great constancy', sharing with the lovers a ritual vision of a life sacramentally informed by love.

Our final example is from *Love's Labour's Lost*. This would seem a classical instance of ritual comedy and so indeed it is, with its withdrawal to an 'academe', its masquings and its concluding débat between winter and spring. But uniquely in this comedy the ritual pattern is transfigured by a tragic glimpse into the 'real' world, a tragic vision that in no way destroys the comedy but raises it to a far higher potentiality. For the mythic material of lovers' reconciliations is following its regular course in comedy, with high preciosity in its wit. Mercade, a courtier enters:

Mercade God save you, Madam!
Princess   Welcome, Mercade,
  But that thou interrupst our merriment.
Mercade I am sorry, Madam, for the news I bring
  Is heavy in my tongue. The king your father –
Princess Dead, for my life!
Mercade Even so. My tale is told.
Berowne Worthies, away! The scene begins to cloud

                                  (V. ii.)

as indeed it does, the sophistication momentarily overborne by the blast of reality. But the play moves to a conclusion in fullest comedy if not in unclouded joy. Troths are still plighted and marriage promised after the play has run its course. And Berowne the scornful (who has nevertheless had the tact to realize the 'clouded scene') is drawn into the troth-plights. He may win his Rosaline but on conditions:

> *Rosaline* You shall this twelvemonth term from day to day
>   Visit the speechless sick and still converse
>   With groaning wretches; and your task shall be
>   With all the fierce endeavour of your wit
>   To enforce the pained impotent to smile.
> *Berowne* To move wild laughter in the throat of death?
>   It cannot be; it is impossible.
>   Mirth cannot move a soul in agony.
>
> (V. ii.)

Out of Berowne's horrified affirmation emerges both a delicately
phrased 'theory of comedy' and a moral issue for Berowne. For
Rosaline generalizes on the nature of wit:

> A jest's prosperity lies in the ear
> Of him that hears it, never in the tongue
> Of him that makes it. Then, if sickly ears,
> Deafed with the clamours of their own dear groans,
> Will hear your idle scorns, continue then,
> And I will have you.
>
> (V.ii.

But Rosaline has measured the wit of his satirical spirit, his 'idl
scorns' and his 'gibing' which is graced only by 'shallow laughin
hearers'. This judgement accepted, Berowne will

> throw away that spirit
> And I shall find you empty of that fault,
> Right joyful of your reformation:

It is lightly, tactfully done and, without impairing the concludin
'songs of Apollo', this subtle gravity following upon the trag
news gives this mannered, 'learned' play a quite unexpecte
dimension.

Our age has considerably lost this Shakespearian sense of ritu
comedy; yet in most unexpected place the ritual act reaffirms its
in the contemporary theatre. There is a certain incongruity

juxtaposing the Shakespearian sense of the 'green world' with the comic practice of Genet and Albee but a valid analogy may be found in the sense of ritual movement. Genet is certainly devoid of the graces of 'other world renewal' in a mythic sense. But in *The Blacks* (London, 1967, Faber and Faber), the exploration of a tragic dilemma, the confrontation of race, is achieved with a ritual intensity and an employment of techniques that are strictly traditional – and the emotional impact is the stronger for this framework. The intention is made clear by Genet's prefatory note:

> This play, written, I repeat, by a white man, is intended for a white audience, but if, which is unlikely – it is ever performed before a black audience, then a white person, male or female, should be invited every evening. The organizer of the show should welcome him formally, dress him in ceremonial costume and lead him to his seat, preferably in the front row of the stalls. The actors will play for him. A spotlight should be focused upon this symbolic white throughout the performance.
>
> But what if no white person accepted? Then let white masks be distributed to the black spectators as they enter the theatre. And if the blacks refuse, then let a dummy be used.
>
> (p. 6)

and this ritual intention is further extended by a passage in the long opening stage direction:

> When the curtain is drawn, four negroes in evening clothes – no, one of them, NEWPORT NEWS, who is barefoot, is wearing a woollen sweater – and four negresses in evening gowns are dancing a kind of minuet around the catafalque to an air of Mozart which they whistle and hum. The evening clothes – white ties for the gentlemen – are accompanied by tan shoes. The ladies' costumes – heavily spangled evening gowns – suggest fake elegance, the very height of bad taste. As they dance and whistle, they pluck flowers from their bodices and lapels and lay them on the catafalque. Suddenly, on the high platform, left, enters the Court. THE COURT. Each actor playing a member of the Court is a masked negro whose mask represents the face of a

white person. The mask is worn in such a way that the audience sees a wide black band all around it, and even the actor's kinky hair.

An audience's unconscious demand for ritual pattern – like a child's demand for ritual game – is here receiving a powerful response in terms of a direct and relatively simple theme. Archibald, one of the principal characters both establishes this sober intention and places it at an ironic distance by two stages which tend to frame the action. In the opening scene he addresses the audience:

> This evening we shall perform for you. But, in order that you may remain comfortably settled in your seats in the presence of the drama that is already unfolding here, in order that you be assured that there is no danger of such a drama's worming its way into your precious lives, we shall even have the decency – a decency learned from you – to make communication impossible. We shall increase the distance that separates us – a distance that is basic – by our pomp, our manners, our insolence – for we are also actors. When my speech is over, everything here – (*he stamps his foot in a gesture of rage*) here! – will take place in the delicate world of reprobation. If we sever bonds, may a continent drift off and may Africa sink or fly away. . . .
>
> (p. 12)

The play pursues its ironic, severely mannered way and Archibald again provides the sardonic frame as the action closes:

> The performance is coming to an end and you're about to disappear. My friends, allow me first to thank you all. You've given an excellent performance. (*The five members of the Court remove their masks and bow.*) You've displayed a great deal of courage, but you had to. The time has not yet come for presenting dramas about noble matters. But perhaps they suspect what lies behind this architecture of emptiness and words. We are what they want us to be. We shall therefore be it to the very end, absurdly. Put your masks on again before leaving. Have them escorted to Hell.
>
> (p. 95)

By the distance, the ironic control of these speeches, a theme fundamentally tragic is given the control and resolution of comedy. This closing comment, moreover, neatly places the renewal of patterned ritual in the theatre into relation with the present dilemma of comedy. 'The time has not yet come for presenting dramas about noble matters.' With the 'death of tragedy' in our day has come the emasculation of comedy, and the theatre proceeds, as Archibald sees his fellows proceed, 'absurdly'. But if themes are rarely 'noble' they are frequently 'significant', of social and moral impact. Albee's *Who's Afraid of Virginia Woolf?*, like Genet's *Blacks*, handles human relationships with ritual intensity in its closing stages. George and Martha ('archetypal Americans' bearing the Christian names of George and Martha Washington) struggle to save their 'campus marriage', with a fantasy child hovering at the edge of their relationship. George realizes that the non-existent 'son' has to be 'killed' if their marriage is to have the prospect of health. At the child's death, and the hysterical despair of Martha, George intones the words from the Requiem Mass, Honey, the helpless neighbour's wife, bearing the responses:

> *Martha* I mentioned him . . . all right . . . but you didn't have to push it over the EDGE. You didn't have to . . . kill him.
> *George* Requiescat in pace.
> *Honey* Amen.
> *Martha* You didn't have to have him die, George.
> *George* Requiem aeternam dona eis, Domine.
> *Honey* Et lux perpetua luceat eis.
> *Martha* That wasn't . . . needed.
>
> [A long silence]
>
> *George* [softly] It will be dawn soon. I think the party's over.
>
>> [May he rest in peace, Amen.
>> Eternal rest grant unto him, O Lord;
>> And let light perpetual shine upon him.]

This is a powerful theatrical moment and it raises some awkward critical questions. Will a sophisticated Broadway or West End audience adequately participate in the serious ironies in this passage, the conjunctions of a mass for the dead with the bitter comedy of a marriage based on fantasy? Is this comedy, despite the laughter, the violent farce, the prospect of a happy resolution? Are the categories of comedy and tragedy here so shattered that we are left with nothing but the very moving, tentative closing page, with its fumbling tenderness:

> *George* [long silence] – It will be better.
> *Martha* [long silence] I don't . . . know.
> *George* It will be . . . maybe.
> *Martha* I'm . . . not . . . sure . . .
> *George* Are you all right?
> *Martha* Yes. No . . .
> *George* Who's afraid of Virginia Woolf . . .
> *Martha* I . . . am . . . George . . . I . . . am . . .

It is a strange historical twist that relates this diversity of ritual moments in the theatre.

7
Certain Relationships of Comedy

> Delight hath a joy in it, either permanent or present.
> Laughter hath only a scornful tickling.
>
> Sir Philip Sidney, *An Apology for Poetry* (1595)

> Eugenius Philolethes [Thomas Vaughan, brother of Henry Vaughan the poet] died as 'twere suddenly when he was operating strong mercurie, some of which by chance getting up into his nose marched him off.
>
> Anthony Wood, ms. note in *Athenae Oxonienses* (1691–2)

Trade Unions are by no means alone in experiencing problems of demarcation and there is a certain embarrassment in treating comedy in a series of monographs including also *The Absurd*, *Irony* and *Satire*. For these are among the delimiting frontiers of comedy and this essay has thus far been so often forced to use the adjectives 'ironic' 'satiric' and 'absurd', that these relationships with comedy had perhaps better be explored, if of necessity briefly. The manuscript entry in a copy of Anthony Wood's *Athenae Oxonienses* at the head of this chapter provides a nice point of entry. The note concerns a sad, indeed tragic fact, the death of Thomas Vaughan while conducting one of his alchemical experiments, with 'strong mercurie'. But the two phrases 'getting up into his nose' and 'marched him off', while indubitably recording the facts, carry with them notes which are by no means tragic. We might suppose on this evidence alone that Wood felt a certain scepticism concerning Vaughan's alchemy and that this irony carried over and modified the fact of its tragic outcome. One is tempted to rank the irony in this modest note as a kind of delicate brutality.

The related modes of absurdity and farce have a similar complexity. This is not the place to explore absurd drama but its conscious ambivalence must be noted as it declares its relations to certain major aspects of comedy. A. P. Hinchcliffe quotes Ionesco on 'the arbitrary nature of dramatic labels' (*The Absurd*, London, 1969, p. 60);

> I have called my comedies 'anti-plays', 'comical dramas' and my dramas 'pseudo-dramas', or 'tragical farces', for, it seems to me, the comical is tragic, and the tragedy of man derisory. For the modern critical spirit nothing can be taken entirely seriously, nor entirely lightly.
>
> (Ionesco, 'Discovering the Theatre', p. 86)

Ionesco's play, *Les Chaises* ends with a note on its music and the final curtain is accompanied in a manner which exactly reflects the ironic confusion of vision in this 'comedy':

> Musique dérisoirement triomphale, de fête foraine, soulignant le jeu ironique, à la fois grotesque et dramatique, des deux acteurs. (Mockingly triumphal music, in the manner of a fair-ground, underlining the ironic action, both grotesque and tragic, of the two participants.)

Hinchcliffe makes a later comment on certain theatrical conventions of absurdist drama which places the tone very precisely:

> ... The use of concrete objects replaces words as a means of communication leading to a new kind of drama, where neither comedy nor tragedy alone can achieve the required and bitter lucidity.
>
> (*The Absurd*, p. 78)

'Objects' on the whole have fewer ambiguities than words and if our aim is 'bitter lucidity', then stage properties may have less indirection than the language of the actors – though, even when we accept this partial truth for the theatre of our own day, we recollect the 'bitter lucidity' of Lear's Fool as he tells him the truth

about himself, and indeed the benign lucidity of Lear at his
reconciliation with Cordelia,

> When you kneel and ask of me a blessing,
> I'll kneel and ask of thee forgiveness –

so near do the language and action of high tragedy approach both
the acrid and happy insights of comedy.

Farce is another matter. If the sense of the absurd finds its most
potent conclusion in the plays of Fernando Arrabal – the performance of *The Car Cemetery* in 1969 revealed the passionate
intensity of his sense of life as a devastated waste-land – farce
reveals its comic power not in the cheerless inanities of *Charlie's
Aunt* but in grave comedy: Feydeau, Chaplin and those farcical
classics of the silent film in which 'things', apparently so merciless,
are defeated by people, in which, from the Keystone Cops to the
Marx Brothers, by way of Mack Sennett and Harold Lloyd, the
diabolical horrors of the machine are circumvented by happy
stupidity or comic endurance. For farce has a serious origin and
intention: it is related to 'farcing' or 'force-meat', that which ekes
out more valuable or significant material, as sausages eke out the
Christmas turkey, or the Ten Commandments are 'farced out' (the
surprising liturgical term) by the 'nine-fold Kyrie' ('Lord have
mercy upon us') and locked up, in the Anglican rite, by the tenth,
longer version of the Kyrie ('Lord have mercy upon us, and write
all these Thy laws in our hearts . . .'). Herrick writes in *Hesperides:*

> As in our clothes, so likewise he who looks
> Shall find much farcing Buckram in our Books

And when the theatre took over the term, farce had a considerable
range of association, as it padded out an evening's entertainment.
It has its powerful analogies in art; in sacred art, in the bitter
comedy of Hieronymus Bosch's minor figures as they gaze at the

central figures in the divine story of Nativity or Passion; in secular art, when the witty obscenities of Jacques Callot throw light on the popular performances of the Commedia dell'Arte as his engravings recapture them in the *Balli di Sfessania*. Among our contemporaries we return to a vivid moment in William Golding's *The Spire*: Jocelin, obsessed by the structure of his cathedral, speaks to Rachel Mason and is shocked into an insight of bizarre comedy, defined in the passage as 'horror and farce':

> What paralysed him was not her spate, but the matter of it, Rachel, face shaken like a windowpane in a gale, was explaining to him why she had no child though she had prayed for one. When she and Roger went together, at the most inappropriate moment she began to laugh – *had* to laugh – it wasn't that she was barren as some people might think and indeed had said, my Lord, no indeed! But she *had* to laugh and then he *had* to laugh –
>
> He stood in sheer disbelief and confusion, until she took herself away into the north ambulatory to catch up with the christening. He stood at the foot of the scaffolding, and part of the nature of woman burned into him; how they would speak delicately, if too much, nine thousand nine hundred and ninety-nine times; but on the ten thousandth they would come out with a fact of such gross impropriety, such violated privacy, it was as if the furious womb had acquired tongue. And of all women in the world, only she, impossible, unbelievable, but existent Rachel would do it – no, be *forced* to do it by some urgency in her spatelike nature, to the wrong person, in the wrong place, at the wrong time. She stripped the business of living down to where horror and farce took over; particoloured Zany in red and yellow, striking out in the torture chamber with his pig's bladder on a stick.
>
> (pp. 59–60)

The lightly-comic obscenity becomes for Jocelin, in his obsessed and enclosed circumstances, farcical horror. We are here very near those moments of 'comedy' where incongruity produces 'sick humour'. We recognize it in the mordant cruelty of the 'interviewer's' question to Abraham Lincoln's widow in the 'sick joke

And tell me, Mrs Lincoln, apart from all that, what did you think of the play?

or in the defensive wit of a friend of mine who wrote in 1940:

> Tell me, where is fancy bread,
> Now that France has fallen?

Farce may be transcended in a further horror – and here neither 'comedy' nor 'tragedy' are terms which fit the case. In Peter Weiss's *The Investigation*, a factual recreation of a war-crime trial, Witness 3 expresses the ironic absurdity by which life – or death – was shaped:

> I myself
> Only escaped gassing
> by accident
> because on that evening
> the ovens were clogged up.

(p. 75)

And Witness 8 describes the prison hospital in terms which recall Bosch or the cruelties of Breughel:

> In the prisoners' hospital it was better.
> There we had bandages of crêpe paper
> some cotton-wool
> a barrel of ointment
> and a barrel of chalk.
> All wounds were painted with ointment
> and for barber's rash we put on chalk
> so you couldn't see it any more.
> We even had a couple of aspirin tablets
> hung on a thread.
> Patients with fever under a hundred
> got to lick them once.
> Patients with fever over a hundred
> were allowed to lick them twice.

(p. 44)

Berowne in *Love's Labour's Lost* protested that whatever 'the fierce endeavour of wit', it was impossible 'to move wild laughter in the throat of death'. It would appear that Peter Weiss's aspirin tablet in the extermination camp has reached even that horror of comedy, a 'wild laughter', which early dramatists rarely conceived.

8

The Aristophanic and Shakespearian Traditions

The argument of this essay should have warned us already against labels and categories, but a certain tradition may be isolated and preserved in the very associations which a literary label gathers to itself. When therefore we name two traditions of comedy 'the Aristophanic' and 'the Shakespearian', we may be doing no more than suggest that a great dramatic genius fathered diverse progeny who bore the same fleeting resemblance to their ancestors that human descendants show; we may also be suggesting that these same giants of comedy established certain main categories within which two very different modes of comedy flourished.

The first mode, the Aristophanic, is an intellectual, analytic and argumentative form, determined with the greatest clarity it can summon, to convince the audience of its thesis. Elder Olson (*The Theory of Comedy*, 1968) declares that all but one 'of the extant eleven plays [of Aristophanes] is comic 'proof' of a single main statement', (p. 73) and he defines the austere economy of means by which this formal end is achieved:

If you want to make dramatic cartoons like those of Aristophanes, you will have to find metaphors which are visual or auditory, and ones that involve actions that can be depicted on the stage. And they will have to be ridiculous – extravagantly so: you can do this by choosing metaphors which debase as much as possible (a kind of inverted hyperbole) without arousing disgust or any serious emotion, and by including the absurd. You will debase and make absurd everything but the likeness which relates the metaphor to the thing you mean; for if you alter that, your whole stratagem fails.

(pp. 71–2)

This is a formal description, a satiric strategy and it depends on a total clarity of aim in the plays of Aristophanes: to deflate war, feminism, literary pretentiousness.

The title of Robert Corrigan's critical study, 'Aristophanic Comedy: The Conscience of a Conservative', defines this social intention, and he goes on to elaborate it:

Because of its concern with society's need and its ability to maintain and preserve itself, comedy is by nature conservative, and Aristophanes and all other writers of comedy tend more or less to be conservatives.

(*Comedy: Meaning and Form*, p. 353)

We may measure this innate drive in Greek comedy of the fourth century B.C. against a similarly conserving instinct in seventeenth-century England. Ben Jonson's *Volpone* moves formally with appalling clarity of means and aim: men are beasts and birds of prey, from their outward manner to their inward natures: Volpone, Voltore, Corbaccio, Corvino. It may be of some greater dignity to be a Fox than a Crow or Vulture, but the condemnation of greed of inordinate battening upon society, identifies all the characters Here then we have a manner which appears to echo Olson's phrase describing the work of Aristophanes: 'dramatic cartoons'. The English tradition of the morality play, its characters identified by their prime characteristics – Perseverance, Good Deeds – seem reinforced by the Jonsonian 'humour', the overriding quality of passion. But examination of the texture of the dramatic verse reveals a greater suppleness than this, without any loss of clarity in the ironic force of the play. At the first speech of the play Volpone is discovered before his hoard of treasure, and the language of his address to it establishes the blasphemous nature of his greed:

> Good morning to the day; and next, my gold!
> Open the shrine, that I may see my saint.

The recess in which the 'piles of gold, plate, jewels' are kept is thus a reliquary ('shrine') enclosing holy things. And the language proceeds in this manner:

> Hail the world's soul and mine!

It is like the first creative word of God bringing light or the pillar of flame that led Israel out of Egypt:

> ... Showst like a flame by night, or like the day
> Struck out of chaos.

His longing for wealth becomes therefore an inordinate worship:

> let me kiss
> With adoration, thee, and every relic
> Of sacred treasure in this blessed room.

His worship proceeds to Faustian lengths:

> The price of souls; even hell, with thee to boot,
> Is made worth heaven.

This is 'comedy' on the edge of a tragic fall, but despite the ambiguity of Volpone's tone, the hard edge of Jonson's irony cuts into the social evil. Later in the play the comedy is ironically broader. In the third act Corvino subjects his wife, Celia, to Volpone's lust in expectation of becoming his heir. Volpone sings lyrically:

> Come, my Celia, let us prove
> While we can, the sports of love,

But with his cry, 'Yield, or I'll force thee', melodrama takes over, to be succeeded by farce as the chaste but ridiculous Bonario leaps out to Celia's defence with the splendidly comic

> Forbear, foul ravisher, libidinous swine!
> Free the forced lady or thou diest, impostor.
> But that I'm loth to snatch thy punishment
> Out of the hand of justice, thou shouldst yet
> Be made the timely sacrifice of vengeance
> Before this altar, and this dross, thy idol.

Volpone *is* a 'libidinous swine', the 'hand of justice' will in the play's conclusion fall heavy on him, his 'idol' is 'dross' and is as much deflated here as in the opening speeches of the play – but the tone has shifted disconcertingly and we are invited to an altogether different comic response from the irony we share with the dramatist in the first scene. And the tone shifts still more sharply at the swingeing sentences passed by the judges in the final scene; here the Aristophanic gravity in social comment rests securely on the many modes of comedy through which this complex play has passed:

> Away with them!
> Let all that see these vices thus rewarded
> Take heart, and love to study 'em. Mischiefs feed
> Like beasts till they be fat, and then they bleed.

It is instructive to compare Jonson's technique with that of Molière whose comedy, in the same tradition of clarity in intellectual power, emerges from a different social milieu. With a preliminary provincial training in the socially-observant improvised farce of the Commedia dell'Arte, Molière came to a Paris dominated by the tragic theatre. His most successful plays were to compete with the brilliance of his contemporary tragedian Corneille, and his closing years extended over the early monumental tragedies of Racine (*Andromaque* was produced at the Hôtel de Bourgogne in 1667; Molière's *Misanthrope* and *Le Médicin malgré lui* appeared in 1666 and *L'Avare* in 1668). These were formidable rivals and nothing less than the complexity and social gravity of Molière's comedy could live with Cornelian and Racinian trag insight. Molière's early plays carried over the delicate satiric wit of the best in the Commedia dell'Arte companies, but as he matured in his craft (both as actor and dramatist), the intensity increases. We recognize again, as in Ben Jonson, the Aristophanic range of social satire, its objects of great diversity: social and intellectual pretensions, religious hypocrisy, covetousness, and a host of minor foibles. But with *Le Misanthrope*, seven years before his death, his art reached perhaps its greatest complexity. For here is a theme, the ultimate rejection of society's corrupt vanity, its failure of compassion and its hypocrisy, which in Shakespeare had produced one of his most acrid tragedies, *Timon of Athens*. The misanthropic Alceste's social attitudes, his violently expressed disgust, lead to a flight from society which parallel Timon's vituperative renunciation of Athenian society. Alceste's closing speech is quite unambiguous:

> Betrayal on all sides, injustice heaped upon me, I mean to escape from this abyss of triumphant vice and search the world for some spot so remote that there one may be free to live as honour bids.

Timon's 'everlasting mansion' by the 'salt sea' reaches the deeper tragic tones which echo *Lear*:

> . . . And nothing brings me all things,

but within the bounds of true comedy, Molière's *Misanthrope* plumbs complex depths rarely achieved in this form of highly intellectual comedy. His recent translator, John Wood writes of his play (Harmondsworth, 1959, p. 11):

> [It] pushes the comic vision of reality to ultimate lengths, or, as some feel, beyond into regions which tragedy alone comprehends. It is a masterpiece of that rare theatre where feeling and intelligence are fused in delight, wise, compassionate, and gay, one of those works, which, as Donneau de Visé put it in words one hesitates to translate, '*font rire dans l'âme.*'

There is little laughter of the heart in *Timon* and the difference in Molière's treatment of the theme is the measure of the austere triumph of the spare, Aristophanic wit in transcending by irony the potentially tragic condition. It is true that the correction of 'vice', whether in *The Frogs*, *Volpone* or *Tartuffe* scarcely mollifies those who are reproved, as Molière ruefully explains in his preface to *Tartuffe* (translated by H. M. Block, New York, 1958):

> Hypocrites do not understand banter; they became angry at once, and found it strange that I was bold enough to represent their actions and to care to describe a profession shared by so many good men. This is a crime for which they cannot forgive me, and they have taken up arms against my comedy in a terrible rage ... Criticism is taken lightly, but men will not tolerate satire.

If Pinter's art of comedy is to be categorized, it belongs here, in the cool intellectual appraisal of insignificant dereliction. Like Beckett, Harold Pinter is not concerned with figures massive enough to bear tragic roles; Davies, Didi and Gogo would be dramatically overwhelmed on Lear's heath. But their hopeless articulation of man's failure to communicate with man is itself a characteristic insight in this tradition of intellectual comedy. Davies's concern to reach Sidcup, in the first act of *The Caretaker*, is a scene of high comedy but its ambiguous omissions and evasions go beyond comfortable laughter:

> *Davies* The weather's so blasted bloody awful, how can I get down to Sidcup in these shoes?
> *Aston* Why do you want to get down to Sidcup?
> *Davies* I got my papers there! They prove who I am! I can't move without the papers. They tell me who I am ... I been going around under an assumed name! That's not my real name.
> *Aston* What name have you been going under?
> *Davies* Jenkins. Bernard Jenkins. That's my name. That's the nam

I'm known by, anyway . . . That's not my real name. If I take that
card along I go in the nick.
Aston What's your real name, then?
Davies Davies, Mac Davies. That was before I changed my
name.

Witty, very good 'theatre' but ironically confounding. What is
Davies's name? What ultimately is the source of his identity? –
behind the laughter there is a total disjunction of spirit.

In those avowed 'Fragments of an Aristophanic Melodrama',
T. S. Eliot's *Sweeney Agonistes*, these questions of human
identity are asked in a darker 'comic' tone. Sweeney makes
his bizarre assault on the emotions of Doris, Snow and the
rest:

> I knew a man once did a girl in
> Any man might do a girl in
> Any man has to, needs to, wants to
> Once in a lifetime, do a girl in.

When pursued into this nightmare world, in which Sweeney gave
the murderer a drink to 'cheer him up', he answers their incredu-
lous 'Cheer him up?' with a declaration of the inadequacy of words
in communication, more explicit than that of Pinter; for Sweeney
says, 'I've gotta use words when I talk to you' more as an evasion
of statement, a declaration of the imprecision of words, than as a
direct expression of simple fact. In this dilemma, words and
existence and identity become meaningless:

> He didn't know if he was alive
>   and the girl was dead
> He didn't know if the girl was alive
>   and he was dead
> He didn't know if they both were alive
>   or both were dead . . .

> When you're alone like he was alone
> You're either or neither
> I tell you again it don't apply
> Death or life or life or death
> Death is life and life is death
> I gotta use words when I talk to you.

If there is laughter in this comedy it is as bitter as any in the history of the theatre.

When we pass from the 'Aristophanic' to the 'Shakespearian' tradition questions of this order are asked with less detached clarity; for we here enter a world not of castigation but of reconciliation, not of reasonable exploration of social follies but of compassionate examination of fallible human relationships. This comedy is not always comfortable; to be in the presence of the Fool can be an unnerving experience, as Orsino and Lear learned. The Fool in Illyria sings 'Come away, Death' in the presence of young lovers and ends a play of twelfth-night revelry with the melancholy certainty that 'the rain it raineth every day'. But those of us who have observed in our own day the insights of Rouault who has brought the same compassionate insight to bear on Christ crucified, the pity and terror of great Kings and the vigorous pathos of the Clown, are little surprised by the stature of the professional court Fool; in whatever circumstances, in the joy of a marriage-masque, in the reconciliation of love in Illyria, in the heart-break of Lear's dereliction, the clown has only one professional concern, to put on his mask, his fool's regalia.

In this comprehensiveness of the comic vision, its refusal to be committed to the clear-cut, Bertolt Brecht plays a notable role. Superficially viewed, Brecht's theatre is 'committed', even didactic ('when I read *Das Kapital*, I understood my plays'), yet nothing could ride more lightly to dogmatic thesis than his great historical plays which treat potential or actual catastrophe or tragedy: the horror of Germany's Thirty Years' War in *Mother Courage* or the persecution and denial of the scientist's integrity in *Galileo*, a failure of nerve which tragically stains the scientist himself. But *Mother Courage* scarcely alludes to the horror of historic fact and the play ends with an ironic parody of a Lutheran chorale:

> Christians, awake! The winter's gone!
> The snows depart, the dead sleep on.
> And though you may not long survive,
> Get out of bed and look alive!

For Brecht consistently declared that the tone of drama should always be governed by *Spass*, by fun, wit or gaiety – 'plays should always be playful' and, as he explains in a note on *Galileo:*

> the more deeply the historical seriousness of a production is established, the more freely can rein be given to humour.

And this is perhaps the secret of 'Shakespearian comedy', the ability in every dramatic situation 'to give rein to humour'. When Parolles in *All's Well* is revealed as a treacherous liar and cheat before all his fellows in the camp he ruefully sets aside excuses and reaches a witty insight into his own condition:

> Even the thing I am shall make me live;

and when Angelo in *Measure for Measure* has been unmasked to such a degree that he himself exclaims:

> So deep sticks it in my penitent heart
> That I crave death more willingly than mercy,

mercy itself, forgiveness and a restoration to human society is given witty expression by the Duke:

> By this Lord Angelo perceives he's safe;
> *Methinks I see a quickening in his eye.*
> Well, Angelo, your evil quits you well.

These categories, 'Aristophanic', 'Shakespearian', or what you will, are rough measure for the subtlety of the individual comedy, yet they answer to some 'family features' which the hindsight of critical history detects in these very various plays. And here, briefly, we may pause to justify the constant preoccupation in this essay with drama. For what, in the exploration of comedy, do we make of Fielding, Jane Austen, Dickens and the whole novel tradition? What of Chaucer, Donne, Pope and the tradition of wit in poetry? For all this is in the realm of comedy and its particular insight. And yet there is a justification for our almost exclusive concern with dramatic comedy – apart from the fact that we borrow the very genre itself from Aristotle's concern for theatrical categories. For drama is swift, compressed and yet exploratory; within its bounds a witty, incongruous situation may be explored concisely with all the irony of Aristophanes or Molière; within the 'two hours traffic' of the stage may also be experienced that often dramatic dimension, when tragic vision is irradiated and intensified by the experience of comedy, so that with Berowne, the comic art extends itself 'to enforce the pained impotent to smile'. In few other arts than this of the theatre is the temper of comedy seen with such diversity and compression.

CONCLUSION

The Metaphysics of Comedy

> Nothing that comes can come amiss,
> No evil, loss or pain. And this
> May be what Plato meant?
>> (F. T. Prince, *Memoirs in Oxford*, 1970)

Miguel de Unamuno, in *The Tragic Sense of Life* ('Salamanca, in the year of grace 1912'), concludes his exploration, as befits a Spanish thinker, with Don Quixote.

> The mortal Don Quixote, in dying, realized his own comicness and bewept his sins; but the immortal Quixote, realizing his own comicness, superimposes himself upon it and triumphs over it without renouncing it.

It is not easy to determine what Cervantes conceived the 'comicness' of Quixote to consist in; what were the windmills against which he tilted and did he, in his comic clumsiness, prevail? Unamuno sees in his comedy symbols of the modern condition:

> But Don Quixote hears his own laughter, he hears the divine laughter, and since he is not a pessimist, since he believes in life eternal, he has to fight, attacking the modern, scientific, inquisitorial orthodoxy ... He fights against the rationalism inherited from the eighteenth century ...
> The world must be as Don Quixote wishes it to be, and inns must be castles, and he will fight with it and will, in all appearances, be vanquished, but he will triumph by making himself ridiculous. And he will triumph by laughing at himself and making himself the object of his own laughter.
>> (Fontana edn., 1962, pp. 311–12)

Unamuno here confirms an intuition to which we have returned throughout this essay, that comedy has its own grave insights and implications, whether in alliance with and within the bounds of tragedy, or on its own independent ground. Many critics have gone further and (like Nathan Scott quoting Fry) speak of the theological bias of comedy:

> So the way of comedy, which attempts to lead us into that special sort of truth which Aldous Huxley calls the 'Whole Truth' – this is a way that is one of the most difficult ways which the modern imagination can be asked to take . . . This, I suspect, is a large part of what Christopher Fry means, when he tells us that 'comedy is an escape, not from truth but from despair: a narrow escape into faith.'
>
> (Nathan Scott, 'The Bias of Comedy' in The *Christian Scholar*, Spring 1961, p. 38, quoting Christopher Fry, 'Comedy', in *Tulane Drama Review*, March 1960, p. 77)

We are here a world (and six centuries) removed from the Dominican Nicholas Trivet who epitomized medieval literary criticism, in commenting on Seneca's tragedies, by approving tragic drama inasmuch as it celebrated the downfall of noble men and dismissed comedy as the treatment of 'the debauching of virgins and the love of prostitutes'. Ours is a more urbane criticism, open to the possibility that laughter has its own sensibility and comedy a metaphysical import. Northrop Frye (in the essay from *The Anatomy of Criticism*, 'The Mythos of Spring: Comedy', already quoted) pursues comedy through its ideal 'five phases'. Passing through the stages of 'ironic comedy', 'Quixote comedy' and 'growing maturity', it reaches its fifth stage when

> it is part of a settled order which has been there from the beginning, an order which takes on an increasingly religious cast and seems to be drawing away from human experience altogether.
>
> (p. 185)

This reminds us of Frye's earlier handling of the 'comedy of the green world', the ideal and regular return for renewal from the sophistication of courts and cities to the 'natural' world, the Arden of the comic vision. But Frye is now prepared to go further. The comedy of the forest of Arden, of Windsor, of Athens of the Dream, is not simply the mythic world of fairy-tale but speaks of a reality beyond myth or folk tale. This is not to say that the pattern of fairy-tale is not a high truth; 'once upon a time ... happy ever after' are childlike and profound phrases. For once, in time, tragedy or misfortune threatened but after great endeavour, Cinderella, Jack, the Princess, the Babes, come out of tragedy into a bliss beyond time – 'and lived happy *ever* after'. Frye's vision of tragedy in its final phase elaborates this basic human instinct in all tale-telling:

> At this point the undisplaced *commedia*, the vision of Dante's *Paradiso*, moves out of our circle of *mythoi* into the apocalyptic or abstract mythical world above it. At this point we realize that the crudest of Plautine comedy-formulas has much the same *structure* as the central Christian myth itself, with its divine son appeasing the wrath of a father and redeeming what is at once a society and a bride.
>
> (p. 185)

These are high words and as we repeat them we may imagine that Will Kempe the Elizabethan jester, Mack Sennett and the Marx Brothers, Chaplin and even Molière, might find their sense of comedy a little overborne by these metaphysical claims. And yet these diverse comic modes, the grotesque, the ridiculous, the ironic, the absurd, the witty jest and the laughter of urbane compassion are all part of a single art, are facets of the nature of Comedy, and they are diverse enough to comprehend metaphysics as well. With this conviction we may allow two friends, whose work in poetry and criticism has made a unique contribution to our contemporary sensibility, to conclude the argument with complementary statements. T. S. Eliot, in his essay 'Poetry and Drama', concludes that all art has the ability to bring us to a condition of serenity, stillness and reconciliation, and then leave us, as Virgil left Dante, to proceed toward a region where that guide can avail us no further.

That region, the goal of the Divine Comedy, is the natural end also of all lesser comedies; but in case we should now adopt too grave a stance for the comic temper, Ezra Pound may remind us, in his *ABC of Reading* that,

Gloom and solemnity are entirely out of place in even the most rigorous study of an art originally intended to make glad the heart of man.

Bibliography

It is more difficult to recommend general reading for the theory of comedy than for tragedy. In the latter case there is a natural starting-point with the *Poetics* of Aristotle; though Aristotle does in fact mention comedy, it is not as central as tragedy to his main argument. None the less, LANE COOPER, in *An Aristotelian Theory of Comedy* (London 1922) establishes the broad classical lines.

If we begin from the questionable basis of a theory of laughter as a major source of comic theory, the most valuable treatment is HENRI BERGSON, *Le Rire: essai sur la signification du comique* (Paris, 1900). Though this is primarily a psychological and philosophical study, the numerous citations from works of literature and criticism from Molière onwards, make it a valuable source-book. SIGMUND FREUD'S *Jokes and their Relation to the Unconscious* is a classical work and was translated and edited by James Strachey (London, 1960). MAX EASTMAN, *The Enjoyment of Laughter* (New York, 1936), extends the psychological study into related fields.

The most 'Aristotelian' of modern literary studies (as one would expect from a leading exponent of the 'Chicago School' of criticism) is ELDER OLSON'S *The Theory of Comedy* (Bloomington Ind., 1968); it goes beyond the promise of its title by giving acute studies of Aristophanes, Plautus, Terence, Shakespeare, Molière and certain 'Moderns'.

There are two outstandingly useful anthologies of critical writing: *Theories of Comedy*, edited by PAUL LAUTER (1964, New York), and *Comedy: Meaning and Form*, edited by ROBERT W. CORRIGAN (San Francisco, 1965) to which this present study is greatly indebted.

Valuable individual studies are: L. J. POTTS, *Comedy* (London,

1949), A. S. COOK, *The Dark Voyage and the Golden Mean* (Cambridge, Mass., 1949), which makes important critical relationships between tragedy and comedy, and I. DONALDSON, *The World Upside Down* (London, 1970). NORTHROP FRYE'S critical works are always provocative and suggestive; his *Anatomy of Criticism* (Princeton, 1957) and *A Natural Perspective* (New York, 1965) contain much matter relating to comedy.

To these more general critical works should be added an important specialist study by ENID WELSFORD, *The Fool, His Social and Literary History* (London, 1935), which remains fresh and stimulating.

Essays by earlier English writers, the critical by-product of their own creative work, are still worth exploring: in particular HAZLITT'S *Lectures on English Comic Writers* (London, 1818) and GEORGE MEREDITH'S *On the Idea of the Comic and the Uses of the Comic Spirit in Literature* (London, 1897). BEN JONSON'S influence was seminal and his dicta and practice are examined in *Ben Jonson:* 'Twentieth-Century Views', edited by J. A. BOUGH (Englewood Cliffs., N.J., 1963), and in *English Stage Comedy*, edited by W. K. WIMSATT (New Haven, 1955). Ben Jonson is so central in this study that his works, with the admirable introductions, should be consulted in the Herford and Simpson edition, together with the following critical studies: E. B. PARTRIDGE, *The Broken Compass* (London, 1958). J. BARISH, *Ben Jonson and Language of Prose Comedy* (Cambridge, Mass., 1960).

It is astonishing that no authoritative and definitive work has been written on Shakespeare's comedies. Much the best general work is J. R. BROWN'S *Shakespeare and His Comedies* (London, 1957). A distinguished work in more limited scope is C. L BARBER'S *Shakespeare's Festive Comedy* (New York, 1959). The Penguin Shakespeare Library contains works of necessary background study and anthologies of critical essays which include examinations of the comedies.

The Restoration period saw a new direction in critical theory and Dryden is the central figure; his *Of Dramatic Poesy and Other Critical Essays* was edited by GEORGE WATSON in 1962 (London). BONAMY DOBRÉE'S *English Restoration Comedy* (London, 1924) is still quite useful but has been superseded by N. N. HOLLAND, *The First Modern Comedies* (Bloomington, Ind., 1959), and by the volume in the Stratford-on-Avon Studies, *Restoration Theatre* (London, 1965), edited by J. R. BROWN and BERNARD HARRIS.

The critical situation concerning modern English drama is confused in many ways; it is impossible to separate English and American experimental work from that of Europe, and it is difficult to distinguish comedy in any traditional meaning of the word from other non-tragic modes, perhaps most comprehensively labelled 'the absurd'. MARTIN ESSLIN'S wide-ranging and acute study, *The Theatre of the Absurd* (Harmondsworth, 1961) gives a clear introduction and a more recent work, J. L. STYAN, *The Dark Comedy* (Cambridge, 1968), amplifies its development. Other studies in the present series (*The Absurd, Burlesque*, etc.) develop the nature of the problem.

For the earlier English comedy of this century much the best approach remains the plays of Bernard Shaw and his own introductions to them. Of more recent writers in the comic theatre, both T. S. Eliot and Christopher Fry have made acute asides, some of which have been quoted in the body of this essay.

Outside the English tradition, the comic theatre in classical Greece and in seventeenth-century France are of the most enduring interest. Much has been written about the former, much of it highly specialist comment on the text, but the following books give the most comprehensive introduction for the general reader:

A. W. PICKARD-CAMBRIDGE, *Dithyramb, Tragedy and Comedy* (London, 1927), on the origins of Greek drama.

GILBERT NORWOOD, *Greek Comedy* (London, 1931), the standard general commentary.

GILBERT MURRAY, *Aristophanes* (London, 1933), a scholarly and readable account of the work.

VICTOR EHRENBERG, *The People of Aristophanes* (Oxford, 1943), a fine survey of the social background to the plays.

There are two useful surveys of the comic spirit in the French theatre:

RENÉ BRAY, *La Préciosité et les Précieux de Thibault de Champagne à Jean Giraudoux* (Paris, 1948), which pursues a fairly constant strain in French comedy.

PIERRE VOLTZ, *La Comédie* (Paris, 1964), a critical history of French comedy from Adam le Bossu to Beckett, and most useful for its anthology of critical passages.

Index